GEOGRAPHY

Curriculum B*ank*

KEY STAGE TWO
SCOTTISH LEVELS C-E

PLACES

SIMON ASQUITH

Published by Scholastic Ltd,
Villiers House,
Clarendon Avenue,
Leamington Spa,
Warwickshire CV32 5PR
Text © Simon Asquith
© 1997 Scholastic Ltd
1234567890 7890123456

AUTHOR
SIMON ASQUITH

EDITOR
LIBBY RUSSELL

SERIES DESIGNER
LYNNE JOESBURY

DESIGNER
CLARE BREWER

ILLUSTRATIONS
MAGGIE DOWNER

COVER ILLUSTRATION
JONATHAN BENTLEY

INFORMATION TECHNOLOGY CONSULTANT
MARTIN BLOWS

SCOTTISH 5–14 LINKS
MARGARET SCOTT AND SUSAN GOW

Designed using Aldus Pagemaker
Printed in Great Britain by Ebenezer Baylis,
Worcester

British Library Cataloguing-in-Publication Data
A catalogue record for this book is available from the
British Library.

ISBN 0-590-53401-7

Contents

ACKNOWLEDGEMENTS

© Material from the National Curriculum, Scottish 5–14 Guidelines and the Northern Ireland Curriculum is Crown copyright and is reproduced by permission of the Controller of Her Majesty's Stationery Office, 1995.

The publishers gratefully acknowledge permission to reproduce the following copyright material:

Ordnance Survey for the use of symbols from *Landranger* map series; Her Majesty's Stationery Office for the adaptation of three maps from the National Curriculum Geography © 1995; © Crown copyright, the Controller of Her Majesty's Stationery Office.

Introduction

Scholastic Curriculum Bank is a series for all primary teachers, providing an essential planning tool for devising comprehensive schemes of work as well as an easily accessible and varied bank of practical, classroom-tested activities with photocopiable resources.

Designed to help planning for and implementation of progression, differentiation and assessment, *Scholastic Curriculum Bank* offers a structured range of stimulating activities with clearly-stated learning objectives that reflect the programmes of study, and detailed lesson plans that allow busy teachers to put ideas into practice with the minimum amount of preparation time. The photocopiable sheets that accompany many of the activities provide ways of integrating purposeful application of knowledge and skills, differentiation, assessment and record-keeping.

Opportunities for formative assessment are highlighted within the activities where appropriate, while separate summative assessment activities give guidelines for analysis and subsequent action. Ways of using information technology for different purposes and in different contexts, as a tool for communicating and handling information and as a means of investigating, are integrated into the activities where appropriate, and more explicit guidance is provided at the end of the book.

The series covers all the primary curriculum subjects, with separate books for Key Stages 1 and 2 or Scottish Levels A–B and C–E. It can be used as a flexible resource with any scheme, to fulfil National Curriculum and Scottish 5–14 requirements and to provide children with a variety of different learning experiences that will lead to effective acquisition of skills and knowledge.

SCHOLASTIC CURRICULUM BANK GEOGRAPHY

The *Scholastic Curriculum Bank Geography* books aim at providing teachers with a comprehensive coverage of the primary geography curriculum. Activities are designed to stimulate the learning and practice of geographical skills according to a range of themes and in the context of a range of places. The books aim to help teachers focus on planning learning in and about their own school's local area, as well as the contrasting localities which have to be taught in these key stages.

There is one book for Key Stage 1/Scottish Levels A–B which provides coverage of early geographical skills using the school grounds and local area, study of a contrasting locality and the thematic study on environmental quality. There are two books for Key Stage 2/Scottish Levels C–E. This one focuses on place study and concentrates on using the local area and learning about contrasting UK and overseas localities, the other concentrates on the themes of Rivers, Weather, Settlement and Environmental Change.

Bank of activities

This book provides a bank of learning activities which may be used in a number of ways. It can be used to supplement existing schemes of work in geography; to supplement a block of work or topic; to help form the framework for a new geography scheme of work (in conjunction with the *Curriculum Bank Geography: Themes* book).

Places to be studied

During Key Stage 2 children should have the opportunity to learn about a wide range of places but it is important that they study a small number in some detail. The National Curriculum requires that children learn about their own locality and two contrasting localities: one in a different part of the

UK, the other overseas. The overseas locality should be in: *'...Africa, Asia (excluding Japan), South America or Central America (including the Caribbean).'* (DfE, 1995 p5)

The National Curriculum also makes it clear that all of these localities should be of a similar size and bases this on the school's locality, saying that this area: *'...will normally contain the homes of the majority of pupils in the school.'* (DfE, 1995 p5)

It is important schools ensure that they can adequately resource teaching about these localities given their detailed and geographically restricted nature.

The National Curriculum requires that thematic studies should include learning about Europe and this is covered directly in the *Curriculum Bank Geography: Themes* book. When schools are deciding which places to study, teachers must take into account that children should be able to answer the following questions about a locality once they have studied it:
▲ Where is this place?
▲ What is this place like and why?
▲ How is the place connected to other places?
▲ What is changing in this place?
... and importantly for children of primary age...
▲ What is it like to be in this place?

Fieldwork

It is essential that fieldwork is a major component of children's learning about places. Knowledge of any place is always more meaningful if it is based on direct experience and it is important that children are provided with experiences which give them opportunities for direct observation and the collection and recording of primary data.

Fieldwork in the local area should under-pin local area studies and occasional visits to other localities are to be encouraged. If the school is able to provide a residential curriculum fieldwork experience during the key stage, it could be the basis for a contrasting locality study and/or a context for thematic studies. Progression through any fieldwork activities should be ensured.

Safety has to be paramount when studying places beyond the school gate. Safety procedures and the teacher's obligations regarding these can be clarified by discussion with the head teacher, checking school policy and local authority guidance. To help the teacher prepare for activities where safety is particularly important, activities where children will be working outside the classroom are flagged with the 📄 icon, and those where they will be outside the school grounds are flagged with the ♣ icon.

Lesson plans

Detailed lesson plans, under clear headings, are given for each activity and provide material for immediate implementation in the classroom. The structure for each activity is as follows:

Introduction

Activity title box

The information contained in the box at the beginning of each activity outlines the following key aspects:

▲ *Activity titles and learning objective* – For each activity, a clearly-stated learning objective is given in bold italics. These learning objectives break down aspects of the programmes of study into manageable, hierarchical teaching and learning chunks, and their purpose is to aid planning for progression. These objectives can be easily referenced to the National Curriculum and Scottish 5–14 requirements by using the overview grids at the end of this chapter (pages 9 to 12).

▲ *Class organisation/Likely duration* – Icons ♀♀ and ⏰ signpost the suggested group sizes for each activity and the approximate amount of time required to complete each one.

▲ *Safety* – Where necessary, safety considerations are flagged with the ⚠ icon.

Previous skills/knowledge needed

Information is given here when it is necessary for the children to have acquired specific knowledge or skills prior to carrying out the activity.

Key background information

This section is intended to help the teacher understand the context of the activity within geographical learning and the geographical concepts under-pinning it. The information should give the teacher greater confidence in teaching the activity.

Preparation

Advice is given for those occasions where it is necessary for the teacher to prime the pupils for the activity; to prepare materials; to set up a display or activity ahead of time.

Resources needed

All of the materials needed to carry out the activity are listed, so that either the pupils or the teacher can gather them together easily before the beginning of the teaching session.

What to do

Easy-to-follow, step-by-step instructions are given for carrying out the activity, including (where appropriate) suggested questions for the teacher to ask the pupils to help instigate discussion and stimulate investigation.

Suggestion(s) for extension/ support

Ideas are given for ways of providing for easy differentiation where activities lend themselves to this purpose. In all cases, suggestions are provided as to how each activity can be modified for the less able or extended for the more able.

Assessment opportunities

Formative assessment suggestions have been included in the 'Assessment opportunities' section. In some of the activities the photocopiable sheet can be used in a summative way. These activities are indicated by the ✍ icon.

Opportunities for IT

Suggestions are made as to how IT might enhance the activity or be directly utilised within it. Regular use of the computer is encouraged for the collection, handling and presentation of data collected as a part of geographical work. Every activity includes suggestions in this section but activities which are particularly relevant to the application of IT are marked with the 🖥 icon, and indicated by the bold page numbers on the chart on page 159. This presents specific areas of IT covered in the activities, together with

more detailed support on how to apply particular types of program.

Display ideas
Where they are relevant and innovative, display ideas are incorporated into activity plans and illustrated with examples.

Other parts of PoS covered
Geography has one Programme of Study (PoS) and one Attainment Target for Key Stage 2. Geographical skills will often be taught through the study of geographical themes in the context of different places; therefore, there is an inevitable (and intended) overlap between different parts of the PoS. The most obvious links are highlighted under this heading.

Reference to photocopiable sheets
Where activities include photocopiable sheets, reproductions of these are included in the lesson plans, together with guidance notes for their use and, where appropriate, suggested answers.

Assessment
This chapter provides assessment activity ideas with accompanying summative assessment sheets. The activities have all been designed to allow the children to do them individually and with little introduction. There are also the some photocopiable sheets from the other chapters which can be used for assessment purposes (see 'Assessment opportunities').

Photocopiable activity sheets
Most of the activities are accompanied by at least one photocopiable activity sheet. Some of these sheets are in direct support of the activity, some form part of the activity, some provide necessary information or techniques and others provide introductory or follow-up opportunities. Many of the sheets have been designed to be generic, allowing any teacher in any school to use them within the context of their own school's local area and the contrasting localities that they decide to study with their pupils.

Cross-curricular links
Strong links between Geography and the Programmes of Study for other subjects of the National Curriculum and Religious Education are identified in a grid (see page 160). In the grid, cross-curricular links with each subject are made with respect to the study of geographical skills, the mapping of places and the study of different localities.

GEOGRAPHY AT KS2: PLACES

Geography is an essential part of every child's education. If taught well it should encourage and develop the natural sense of wonder that young children have about the world in which they live. It should help children find answers to their questions about the world and it should stimulate a desire for ever-increasing knowledge and understanding of the world and the people in it.

This book is concerned with places, with the people who inhabit those places and with the interaction between people and place. In primary school, the topic of Geography should involve children in asking questions and exploring real issues surrounding the human and physical worlds and how those worlds inter-relate.

Geography investigates the spatial dimension and the patterns and processes operating within space. It is concerned with the spaces between places and how these places are linked together. It is a vehicle for improving empathy between different cultures and understanding why the world is as it is.

In learning about geography children will be observing, recording, analysing, and presenting and communicating their findings to others. This will lead to the development of their interpersonal and group work skills.

This book encourages the teacher to truly 'involve' the children in their world and in the issues operating within it. It enables children to move out of the classroom and to examine the world first hand and it encourages teachers to help children make sense of their world by developing their skills and providing as meaningful a range of experiences of other places as possible.

The book aims to show that with a little forward planning, places can be presented to children as 'real' and not simply abstract areas of knowledge beyond their direct experience. It asks that the 'key questions' identified at the beginning of the book be seen as centrally important to planning and resourcing teaching about places.

It is important to support the development of children's attitudes and values as well as their knowledge, skills and understanding. The activities provided in this book can be used to provide children with as accurate an understanding as possible about what it would be like to live in the places that they study closely and to provide them with an overview of the world as a whole.

Overview grid

Learning objective	PoS/AO	Content	Type of activity	Page
Skills in the study of places				
To develop an ability at describing and interpreting the children's own surroundings.	3a *Aspects of the physical and built environment P4–P6*	Describing real places in classroom/grounds. Using adjectives.	Pairs in a group. Classroom/grounds activity.	14
To develop the appropriate use of vocabulary in a geographical context.	3a *As above*	Matching words to pictures.	Small group matching game.	15
To measure the air temperature using a thermometer as part of a fieldwork exercise.	3b **Science: Energy** – *Properties and uses of energy P4–P6*	Measuring air temperature. Fieldwork skills. Data handling.	Pairs in groups. Fieldwork in grounds. Classroom data handling.	17
To learn to interpret photographs as secondary sources.	3e *Aspects of the... environment P4–P6*	Photograph interpretation.	Small group photograph interpretation game.	19
To use IT to assist in the handling and presentation of geographical data.	3f **IT: Uses** – *Techniques for using computer software P4–P6*	Creating computer spreadsheet using data on distances children live from school.	Group work. Pairs at computer. Interpreting map scale; data handling using IT.	20
Mapping places				
To make plans and maps of the children's own school environment showing an appreciation of the benefits of working at different scales.	3c *Making and using maps P7–S2*	Relationship between detail and area covered in different scales of maps.	Group discussion. Individual worksheet mapping activity based on table top, classroom and school.	24
To use and interpret maps at a variety of scales.	3d *As above*	Identifying detail and coverage of different scales of maps of the same place.	Individual map work.	25
To make a map of the school and to remap it at a different scale.	3c *As above*	Mapping of school building(s). Remapping at a different scale.	Individual mapping scale work using squared paper.	27
To add symbols to a map following field sketching in the school locality.	3c *As above*	Fieldwork observation and recording skills. Class-based mapping of information.	Small group walk in local area. Class-based mapping task.	28
To understand the eastings before northings convention in the use of co-ordinates.	3d *As above*	Teaching/reinforcement of the eastings before northings convention in grid location.	Whole class or group memory game.	30
To develop an understanding of the four-figure grid reference system.	3d *Making and using maps P4–P6*	Mapping using the four-figure grid referencing system.	Individual worksheet grid referencing activity.	32
To understand the purpose of the four points of the compass.	3d *As above*	Work on four main compass points. Relating this to globe. Researching places in each direction.	Group discussion and research work using globe.	33

GEOGRAPHY KS2: PLACES

Learning objective	PoS/AO	Content	Type of activity	Page
To be able to measure direction using the four points of the compass.	3d *Making and using maps P4–P6*	Following routes using the four points of the compass.	Discussion in group. Paired route-making and following.	35
To be able to measure distance using a map with a scale.	3d *As above*	Discussion about measuring distance on maps. Mapping activity.	Individual worksheet map work. Measuring distance using map scales.	37
To be able to use a map to set and follow a route.	3d *As above*	Creating and following routes.	Group work. Designing trails. Following trails.	39
To be able to use an atlas to assist with studies. To be able to use the contents and index page of an atlas.	3d *As above*	Finding information about places by using the contents/index pages of an atlas.	Paired atlas referencing work. Children challenge each other.	41
To have a basic knowledge of the UK and to be able to identify certain features on a UK map.	3d *As above*	Gaining a basic knowledge of the points of reference on KS2 map A.	Story writing by individuals. Map work.	42
To have a basic knowledge of Europe and to be able to identify certain features on a map of Europe.	3d *As above*	Gaining a basic knowledge of the points of reference on KS2 map B.	Individual design of travel advertising posters.	44
To have a basic knowledge of the world and to be able to identify certain features on a world map.	3d *As above*	Gaining a basic knowledge of the points of reference on KS2 map C.	Group quiz design activity based on world points of reference.	47
Studying your locality				
To appreciate the extent of your school's locality.	4 *As above*	Defining the school's locality and mapping it.	Individual mapping and worksheet activity.	50
To recognise the physical features of your school's locality.	5a *Aspects of the environment... P4–P6*	Observation of locality's physical features. Recording information and ideas by drawing.	Whole class walk. Follow up individual drawing activity.	52
To understand the range of human features which provide the children's locality with its character.	5a *Ways in which places have affected people... P4–P6*	Consideration of main human features in local area.	Individual designing of guide book front covers.	53
To recognise the importance of environmental issues in giving your locality its character.	5a *Locations, linkages and networks P4–P6*	Collecting data of travel methods and preferred travel methods. Handling and presenting the data.	Whole class data collection, handling and presentation activity comparing children's actual and preferred methods of journeying to school.	55
To recognise that human activities in your locality relate to its features.	5c *Making and using maps P4–P6*	Consideration of services in their local area.	Map drawing and individual design and justification of bus routes.	57

**GEOGRAPHY
KS2: PLACES**

Learning objective	PoS/AO	Content	Type of activity	Page
To recognise and to be able to explain what is changing in your locality.	5d *Ways in which places have affected people... P4–P6*	Consideration of issues to do with change in the local area.	Small group newspaper design activity.	58
To understand the complex links your area has with other places.	5e *Locations, linkages and networks P4–P6*	Mapping and analysis of transport links around your local area at different scales.	Individual map reading and tracing activity.	60
There are similarities and differences between your locality and other localities.	5b *Aspects of the environment... P4–P6*	Identification of positive characteristics of two localities.	Pairs creating posters to advertise the two localities.	62
To recognise characteristics of the local area concerned with rivers, weather, settlements and environmental change.	6 *As above*	Identification of features to do with the four KS2 themes in children's own locality.	Class discussion and group creation of parts of a whole class collage.	63
Studying a contrasting UK locality				
To show that there is an enormous variety of places in the UK.	4 *As above*	Accessing information on places in the UK using reference books and atlases.	Paired reference work using books and completion of worksheet.	66
To recognise the physical features of a contrasting locality in the UK.	5a *As above*	Identification of physical features using photographs. Drawing and discussion of drawings.	Group work. Each child redraws a picture identifying physical features. Group discussion.	67
To recognise human features in a contrasting UK locality.	5a *Ways in which places have affected people... P4–P6*	Consideration of jobs carried out in the locality and what they entail.	Paired questions game. Written work on what it would be like to do a job in the locality.	69
To explore and communicate an important environmental issue to others in a contrasting UK locality.	5a *As above*	Reporting different views on a real environmental issue in the locality.	Small group writing and recording of a 'radio programme' article using a tape recorder. Whole class putting together and listening to completed 'programme'.	71
To appreciate the connection between the features of a contrasting UK locality and the human activity within it.	5c *As above*	Mapping work on the locality. Identification of physical and human features which help account for the location of other features.	Individual tracing of maps and completion of worksheet.	73
To understand some of the important changes operating in a contrasting UK locality.	5d *As above*	Consideration of changes to how the locality looks.	Individual worksheet drawing activity.	74
To be able to connect the contrasting UK locality with other parts of the British Isles using a map.	5e *As above*	Use of atlases to identify places studied and major connecting communication routes.	Individual/group/class atlas and worksheet activity.	76

**GEOGRAPHY
KS2: PLACES**

Learning objective	PoS/AO	Content	Type of activity	Page
To recognise the similarities and differences between your contrasting UK locality and your own locality.	5b *Ways in which places... P4–P6* *Making and using maps P4–P6*	Creating land use maps for the two localities. Comparison of the maps.	Individual colouring in of land use classifications on maps of two localities. Written explanations of comparison of two maps.	77
To create an information bank about your own locality.	6 *Recording and presenting P4–P6*	Collection of information on the four KS2 themes.	Groups research one theme. Class sharing of information.	79
Studying a contrasting overseas locality				
To be able to put places studied in the course of their school work into a world context.	4 *Collecting evidence P4–P6*	Gathering information about a range of world locations.	Paired research work in groups. Sharing of information.	82
To consolidate knowledge of some of the world's major physical features. To put contrasting overseas localities studied into a world context.	5a *As above*	Identification of major physical features using a map and atlas.	Individual/paired atlas and worksheet activity.	83
To compare features in your own settlement and a contrasting overseas settlement.	5a *Aspects of the environment... P4–P6*	Identification of skylines typical of the locality being studied.	Group work following class/group discussion. Drawing, cutting out and sticking activity.	85
To recognise that there are important environmental issues for people living in a contrasting overseas locality.	5a *Ways in which places have affected people... P4–P6*	Listening to viewpoints and going in to role as part of a debate. Monitoring and recording of main lines of argument in a debate.	Whole class debate on environmental issue. Group discussion and presentation of a line of argument. Written recording of debate.	87
To recognise the relationship between physical and human features in a contrasting overseas locality.	5c *As above*	Identification of major physical and human features in a locality. Identification of relationships between these features.	Papier mâché model-making in groups. Group discussion.	89
To demonstrate an understanding of the communication links between the overseas locality being studied and your own locality.	5e *Locations, linkages and networks P4–P6*	Identification of routes between localities studied using atlases.	Individual/group worksheet and atlas activity.	90
To consider similarities and differences between your locality and a contrasting overseas locality.	5b *Aspects of the environment... P4–P6*	Identification of key visual characteristics of your locality and the contrasting locality.	Whole class activity. Creation of a joint 'coat of arms' for the 'twinned' localities.	91

Entries given in italics relate to the Scottish 5–14 Guidelines.

GEOGRAPHY
KS2: PLACES

Skills in the study of places

Children studying geography at Key Stage 2 should be learning about geographical themes while using geographical skills in the context of places. To study places they need to use a wide range of skills, in particular those skills which are associated with fieldwork, using secondary sources, Information Technology and mapping. Skills range from those which are specifically relevant to work in the school and its locality to those relevant to studying distant places of which they may not have first hand experience.

Skills associated with other curriculum areas are relevant to geography. For example, mathematical skills to do with counting, shape, measuring and graphing; and science and language skills surrounding observation, questioning, recording and communicating.

Information Technology is of increasing consequence in the teaching and learning of geography in terms of the provision of information, the presentation of findings, the storage and handling of data and communication. Computer skills can be used in many of the activities.

Many of these activities can be used across a wide range of scales and contexts and involve children in recognising pattern across space and answering key geographical questions. The activities here are based on children having direct experience where possible so that their learning is meaningful and relevant to them. Several activities, therefore, promote the idea of taking children out of the classroom. A full risk assessment under guidance from the school must be carried out prior to these activities.

13

DESCRIBING PLACES IN OUR SCHOOL

To develop an ability to describe and interpret the children's own surroundings.

†† *Pairs within a group.*

🕐 *30 minutes for the discussion and classroom activity; 20 minutes for fieldwork around school; 10 minutes discussion for follow-up.*

Previous skills/knowledge needed

The children should be familiar with the extent of the school buildings and grounds which are within 'bounds'. They should know how to use a simple chart to record information. Some simple work on adjectives may prove useful beforehand.

Key background information

Opportunities to explore the school buildings and grounds for exploration's sake should have been encouraged at an early stage. Now you should be beginning to ask children to describe and interpret their surroundings as well. It is important to understand the progression in the children's knowledge of their surroundings from awareness to exploration through to description and then interpretation.

Preparation

Think about the range of adjectives which might be used to describe the classroom or a part of it. Write these words on to cards. Enlarge photocopiable page 100 to help you introduce the activity.

Resources needed

A board, pens or chalk (for a brainstorming session), an enlarged version of the photocopiable sheet on page 100, enough copies of the photocopiable sheet for each pair, clipboards or alternatives, pencils, bank of cards (for support).

What to do

Ask the children to circulate around the classroom and think of as many words to describe their classroom as possible. Suggest that they use their five senses to explore the room. Bring the children together and get them to spend a few minutes brainstorming words while you write them down on the board. Help them to agree on six different adjectives which describe the room well. Write the adjectives on to the

enlarged photocopiable sheet and ask the children to give reasons why these words describe the room, filling in the right hand side of the chart. The children should be encouraged to see that general forms of description (for example, smelly) are less useful than small phrases (for example, smells of polish). With some children it will be worth questioning whether 'polishy' is a good word, while with others it may deserve strong praise.

The 'Why?' side of the chart might contain explanations such as 'because the classroom gets cleaned every evening'.

Having practised this exercise in the classroom, give each pair a photocopiable sheet on a clipboard and a pencil and send them to find a location within the school grounds. They should fill in the 'What is your place like?' column of the chart at their chosen location but could complete the 'Why'? column of their return to the classroom.

A reporting back session could be followed by a discussion of the range of differing locations around the school.

Suggestion(s) for extension

Rather than working in groups or pairs, ask each child to complete the second part of the activity separately. Issues of personal viewpoints as well as accuracy and quality of interpretation will then be highlighted.

Children can be led into suggesting which places are the most 'opposite'. Are there some places which are similar in some ways but opposite in others?

Suggestion(s) for support

A bank of cards with adjectives written on them can be useful for those children who struggle to access words from their own vocabulary. Alternatively, a dictionary list of adjectives on one sheet would do the same job and have the advantage that the child could take it to the place considered. Pair the children so that more confident ones support those who are less confident.

Assessment opportunities

Encouraging the children to use as many describing words as they can, ask them to report back on the place they studied. Log any words they use which you consider specific to geographical work (such as temperature, environment, pollution, wildlife area and leisure). This could provide evidence that they can use geographical vocabulary to describe and interpret their surroundings.

Skills in the study of places

The photocopiable sheet "Our School" worksheet shows:
Name _____ Our School _____ Date _____
Our place
What is your place like? Write six describing words or phrases in these boxes
Why? What reasons do you have for choosing these words?
(with boxes numbered 1–6, surrounded by words: concrete, leafy, noisy, boring, muddy, grass, exposed, cold, calm, pretty, grey, quiet, natural, tarmac, green, warm, attractive, sheltered, busy, ugly, exciting, favourite)

Opportunities for IT

The children could use a tape recorder to collect and explain the adjectives they have chosen. They could use a word processor, desktop publishing program or spreadsheet to make a tabular form of the 'Why' and 'What is your place like' columns. If the children use a word processor for this they will need to be shown how to use the TAB settings, or hanging indent to set up the columns. For example:

Smells of polish   *Because the classroom gets cleaned every morning*

The children could go on to word process a description of the place using the selected adjectives.

Display ideas

Children can draw pictures or even make collages using real materials from the places which they have studied. Each pair could follow up the activity by enlarging the photocopiable sheet and illustrating each of their 'What is your place like?' sections. The children's work can be displayed alongside photographs of the places studied. If the school has a camera, then the children could take the photographs themselves.

Other aspects of the Geography PoS covered

2a, b, c; 3b.

Reference to photocopiable sheet

The photocopiable sheet on page 100 can be used by the children to write their describing words (in the 'Why?' column) and to explain why each adjective is relevant (in the 'What is your place like?' column). It should be emphasised to children that this sheet represents a structured way to collect information and present findings. The sheet can be enlarged in order to help introduce the activity and to enable the children to illustrate their findings.

USING THE RIGHT WORDS

To develop the appropriate use of vocabulary in a geographical context.

†† *Individuals, then small groups.*

🕐 *10 minutes explanation; 15–20 minutes to fill out the photocopiable sheet; 20 minutes to play the game.*

Previous skills/knowledge needed

Children must be capable of working collaboratively and must have an appropriate reading vocabulary.

Key background information

Children should be beginning to realise that there is an appropriate, 'technical' vocabulary associated with geographical work. These involve:

▲ words which describe position, location and movement;

▲ names for geographical things, such as 'mountain' or 'dual carriageway';

▲ technical words such as 'temperature' or 'latitude'.

An expanding vocabulary will help the children to describe places and use more precise reasoning in their work.

'rough', for example, may offer 'Sometimes the sea can be very rough in the harbour.' If the flashcard has been 'summit' a weak child may not offer a sentence while a stronger child might come up with 'The harbour was a long way below the summit of the nearest mountain.' If a child cannot think of a suitable sentence to describe the picture, then the child sitting on the right can have a go with the same card. Having incorporated their chosen word into a spoken sentence correctly a child can then keep the flashcard. The child who ends up with the most flashcards wins the game.

Preparation

Collect a range of images of places and make a display for the class. These images can be either related to an area of work you are doing as a class or simply a general collection of pictures. Make a bank of 'flashcard' labels, several of which should be appropriate for each of the images, and place them face down in the centre of a table. The flashcard labels could be word processed. Photocopy the sheet on page 101 for each child in the class.

As an alternative to displaying the images on the wall you could mount each of the images on card and make them into work cards which could be used in table-top fashion.

Resources needed

A collection of images (posters, magazine photographs) showing a range of places, a collection of flashcards, a copy of the photocopiable sheet on page 101 for each child in the group, pencils or crayons.

What to do

Prior to playing the game, use the photocopiable sheet on page 101 to introduce the idea of matching words and images. Give each child in the class a copy of the sheet and a pencil or crayon. They are to draw a line from each picture to the word which best describes it.

Explain that the point of the activity is to see which words are best to describe places. Then, seat the children in groups so that everyone can see the display of images easily and ask each child to choose an image. The children take turns to choose one of the flashcards from the pile of face-down cards in the centre of the table. Having chosen a card, each child makes up a sentence using the word and describing the picture he has chosen in some way. A child who has chosen a photograph of a Scottish fishing village, and has picked the flashcard

Suggestion(s) for extension

You could provide flashcards with a mixture of words which are easy to place (for example, high and big) and words which are more difficult to use (for example, summit, waterfall and junction). More difficult words could be mounted on yellow card and worth two points while the less difficult words could be mounted on red card and worth one point.

Suggestion(s) for support

Sets of flashcards which are graded according to difficulty can be used with children of different abilities. Group the children according to their ability and give each group a set of cards suitable for their level. Children could record their ideas on tape.

Assessment opportunities

Sit with the group and assess each child's skill in using the words appropriately. The photocopiable sheet on page 101 could provide a written record of adjective choice. Children could be asked to write sentences using the words on the back of the sheet.

Opportunities for IT

Children could use a word processor to make the flashcards for use in the game, as well as to write out their sentences.

Display ideas

Incorporate the flashcards in the display of place pictures. If children have word processed their sentences, these could also be displayed.

Other aspects of the Geography PoS covered

3e; 4; 5a.

Reference to photocopiable sheet

The photocopiable sheet on page 101 requires children to link pictures with appropriate geographical vocabulary.

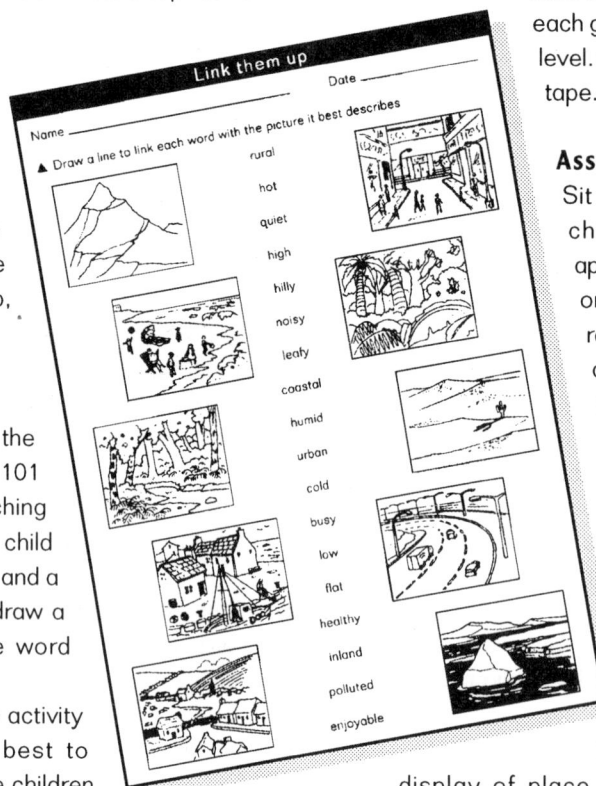

MEASURING TEMPERATURE

To measure the air temperature using a thermometer as part of a fieldwork exercise.

†† *Groups which can be sub-divided into pairs.*

🕐 *15 minutes for the classroom activity; 15 minutes for the field activity in school grounds; 15 minutes for the final classroom activity.*

Previous skills/knowledge needed

Children will need to be capable of filling in a simple table and will be required to read a thermometer.

Key background information

Temperature can differ greatly from place to place even within quite small distances. Variations in temperature around the school grounds can be linked with site conditions, for example shelter from the wind afforded by surrounding vegetation may raise temperatures slightly. Fieldwork skills such as identifying study sites, reading a thermometer, recording data and then interpreting that data are centrally important to a geographer.

Preparation

Each child will require a copy of the photocopiable sheet on page 102. Each group will need to use three or four small, movable thermometers (safe versions are available through most educational stockists). It is worth spending some time considering places in your grounds which might provide different temperature readings.

Resources needed

A copy of the photocopiable sheet on page 102 for each child, three or four thermometers per group, clipboards or alternatives, pencils, a map of the school grounds may also be helpful.

What to do

Discuss with the class that although we talk about 'a cold day' or 'a warm day', temperatures on that day can still vary from one place to another. Make sure that all the children know how to read the temperatures on a thermometer correctly.

Divide the class into groups and give each child a copy of the photocopiable sheet. Ask each group to choose three or four places outside where they think temperatures might be different. Each group writes down on their sheet where each place is and notes which place they think will be the warmest and which the coolest. Pairs from the group then each go to one of the places, measure the temperature and record the results. Once all of a group's pairs have returned to the classroom, the children can swap information and fill in their photocopiable sheets with the temperatures from the different places.

Having recorded their data, the children now try to interpret it. Get them to write their explanations for why certain places are warmer or cooler at the bottom of the sheet. Ask the children whether their initial guesses were correct. Complete the activity with a class discussion, using the map of the school grounds to raise these questions:

▲ Which is the warmest place in the school grounds?
▲ Which is the coldest place in the school grounds?
▲ Are there any places where the characteristics of the landscape and buildings might be responsible for the temperatures recorded? 'Wind tunnels' for example, might cause a lowering of temperatures; the lee side of a building might record a higher temperature; there may be 'sun traps'.
▲ Do the children think that there might be very different recordings on different days, at different times of the day or at different times of year?

Suggestion(s) for extension

Ask the children to explain their initial guesses about which locations will be the warmest or coolest before they go outside. This will encourage them to make educated guesses and help them to consider the factors which are likely to affect temperature.

Suggestion(s) for support

Use a map to show children the school grounds and to help explain some of the variations in temperature. If the children are helped by seeing their data drawn in mapped form, you could look at all the places chosen by the class as a whole and map them using colours for different ranges of temperatures.

Skills in the study of places

Assessment opportunities

The completed photocopiable sheet will provide an opportunity to assess the children's ability to draw conclusions about their own locality with respect to factors affecting temperature. Back up the evidence provided by these sheets with observation during the class reporting back session or by observation during each group's discussion.

Opportunities for IT

The children could use a spreadsheet to record the temperatures they have taken and the place. They might also include a directional and description column. For example:

	a	b	c	d
1	Place	Facing	Temperature	Details
2	Entrance	South	15°C	in direct sunlight
3	Infants entrance	North	10°C	in shade
4			AVE(C2,C3)	

The spreadsheet could be used to work out the average or extreme temperatures. Graphs could be plotted using the Facing/Place and Temperature columns. Alternatively, the same fieldnames could be used to create a database.

If the school has access to data-logging equipment children can either use a hand data-logger or a temperature probe linked to the computer to log automatically the temperature. Data from a hand data-logger can be fed back into the computer once in the classroom. An interesting extension to this activity is to set up the data-logging equipment to record the temperatures at regular intervals across the day, and even night. The results can be shown on the computer screen in the form of a graph. The children can then interpret the graph, identifying, for instance, the way that the temperature rises and falls as the sun reaches and leaves the place, or that the temperature fell when it rained in the middle of the day. Over the week different places could be selected and the graphs compared.

An important aspect of this work is to ensure that the children appreciate the use of the technology and discuss where these types of applications have important uses outside of school.

Display ideas

If enough places have been sampled by the class as a whole, you could make a very effective temperature chart based on the large scale map of the school, colouring areas with temperatures in the same band.

Other aspects of the Geography PoS covered
2b, c; 4.

Reference to photocopiable sheet

Children use the photocopiable sheet on page 102 to record this activity, list their sample sites, write down their predictions, record their results and explain them. The sheet can also be used for assessment purposes.

WHAT'S IN THE PICTURE?

To learn to interpret photographs as secondary sources.

†† *Small groups.*

🕐 *5 minutes for the explanation; 15–20 minutes to do the introductory activity on the photocopiable sheet; 20–30 minutes for the group activity.*

Previous skills/knowledge needed

The children will need simple drawing and recording skills.

Key background information

First hand experience always provides the best learning opportunities for young children. Secondary sources give 'second hand' information. Pictures, along with books, are perhaps the most commonly used secondary sources in the primary classroom. Although pictures are widely used they rarely fulfil their potential. Pictures can be 'interrogated' to find out as much information as possible.

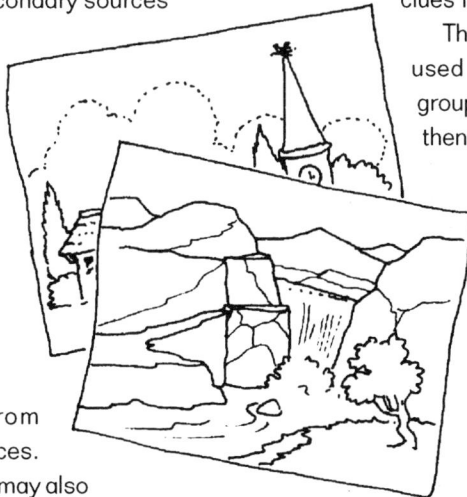

Preparation

Collect a variety of images from magazines, posters or similar sources. Mount them on to backing card. You may also want to protect them with transparent, adhesive plastic and cut them into two (or more) pieces to make a sort of jigsaw. At least one piece of key information about the scene portrayed should be absent when one of the pieces is removed. You could cut selected 'holes' in the image, cut the picture in half, possibly using a zigzag fashion. Make sure that you label the backs of the pieces in each set so that no pieces are lost. Make copies of the photocopiable sheet on page 103 for each child.

Resources needed

Picture resources mounted on to backing card, a copy of the photocopiable sheet on page 103 for each child, plain and coloured pencils.

What to do

Introduce the activity by giving each child a copy of the photocopiable sheet on page 103. Each child secretly draws in what they think is missing from the four blank spaces and then the group shares their different ideas. Emphasise any variety in the interpretations and give particular credit to attempts made by children who have 'read' the clues in the rest of the picture.

The 'picture card sets' you have made are best used with children who are working in small groups. Give each child a part of a picture and then ask them to write down what they think is missing. Encourage them to look very carefully at the pictures to see if they can find any clues. Children could be encouraged to look carefully by asking:

▲ Are there any lines which run into the missing part of the photograph?

▲ Are there any reflections of things which are in the missing piece?

▲ Do things in the missing piece cast any shadows?

▲ Are there any activities going on which give any clues?

Ask each child to tell the rest of the group what they think is missing. The rest of the group could now make their own guesses. Once everyone has made their guesses give out the missing pieces of the pictures. It is fun to operate a scoring system where children who correctly guessed their own picture get two points and children who correctly guessed other people's pictures get one point.

**GEOGRAPHY
KS2: PLACES**

If you wish to use the activity with the whole class you could get each group to challenge another group.

Suggestion(s) for extension
Ask the children to list specific clues to help them to identify what is in the missing part of their picture. Encourage geographical observation with respect to human and/or physical features contained in the first piece of each picture.

Suggestion(s) for support
Differentiate this task by making some of the cut-outs easier to guess than others or by making sets of 'picture card sets' suitable for children at different levels.

Assessment opportunities
This activity provides an excellent assessment opportunity. Sit with each group and listen to their comments and explanations for their guesses. If the children have written down their guesses you could annotate their writing. Look particularly for evidence of each child's ability to interrogate the photograph as a secondary source.

Opportunities for IT
Children could be set the task of using a camera to make their own version of the activity for their local area by taking photographs around the school's locality. They can then 'try out' their photograph jigsaws on another group or class.

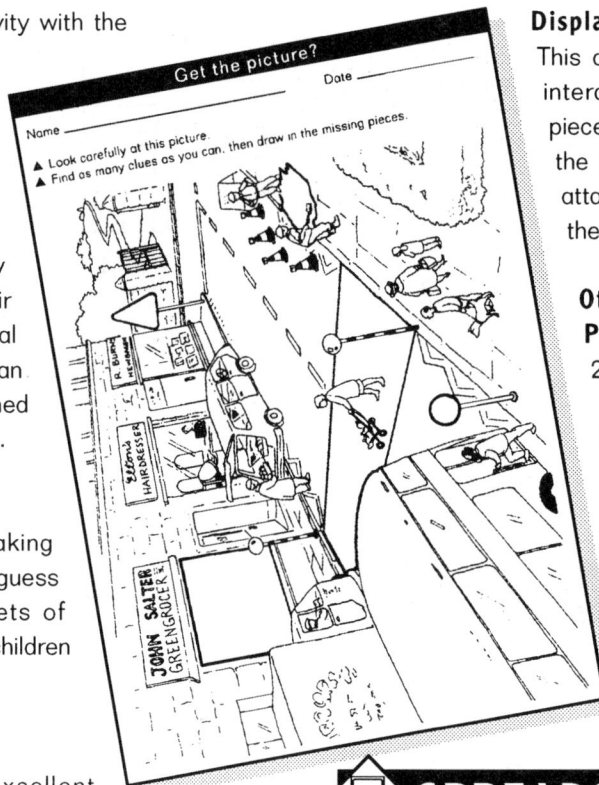

Display ideas
This activity provides a most effective interactive display. Mount the larger pieces of picture on the wall and provide the missing pieces on a table top (or attached to the wall by thread). Invite the children to match the pieces.

Other aspects of the Geography PoS covered
2a; 3a; 4.

Reference to photocopiable sheet
The photocopiable sheet on page 103 should be used to introduce the photograph/jigsaw activity. Children draw what they believe is missing in the five 'holes' in the picture of a street scene.

SPREADSHEET PRESENTATION

To use IT to assist in the handling and presentation of geographical data.

†† *Groups within the class (divided into pairs at the computer).*

⏲ *15 minutes introduction to group; 20 minutes map activity; 5–10 minutes per pair at the computer to input data; 5–10 minutes per pair at the computer to create a graph and print out; 15 minutes for graphing on paper (optional).*

Previous skills/knowledge needed
This activity involves children in using a spreadsheet program on their class computer. Children should be able to use a simple map of their school and the local area and be capable of recording simple information. They should also have been introduced to simple graphing skills.

Key background information
A spreadsheet is a simple way to organise data and information. To input information the operator simply clicks on cells in a matrix either using the mouse or keyboard arrows and types in the numbers or words which make up the information.

Preparation
Acquaint yourself with the spreadsheet program most suited to the computer you will use. Make sure that the program will work with numeric data and that it is capable of creating

simple graphs. Many spreadsheet programs have simple and quick graphing facilities (for example: Microsoft, Excel's 'Chart Wizard', Longman's Advantage program or Claris Work's 'Spreadsheet' option).

Prepare a large scale map of your local area which includes as many of the children's homes as possible.

Resources needed
A large scale local map, paper and pencils, computer with a spreadsheet program, a copy of the photocopiable sheet on page 104 for each child.

What to do
Gather the children around the map of your 'catchment area' and help each child to identify where his or her home is shown. Ask them to take it in turn to use paper and pencil to help them calculate the distance that they live from school. The illustration on page 22 indicates how to do this.

One side of a piece of paper is positioned along the start of the route from the child's home and a pencil mark is made across the map and the paper to mark their house. Another pencil mark is made at the first bend in the route and the paper is then turned to line up with the rest of the route and a mark is made at the next bend. This process is repeated until the whole route has effectively been 'straightened' along the side of the paper. The child then uses the scale on the map to calculate the length of the journey.

Having measured the distance from their home to school, each child types their name into the first column of cells in the spreadsheet program and their distance in the second column. Once each child has inputted their name and distance they collect information from their classmates and

add this data below their own in the spreadsheet. They then select all the name and distance cells and use the graphing facility (usually operated by clicking a menu button) to produce a line graph showing the distances for each child. The children can quickly learn to set their graphs out in different ways.

It is important to 'save' each graph created by a different child. Show each child how to write their own name on the graph or on the spreadsheet printout.

Encourage the children to make their own (long hand) table (see page 22 for an example) and use photocopiable sheet 104 to support the important concepts and procedures involved in compiling tables and graphs, particularly if a computer is not available.

Suggestion(s) for extension
Children may realise that their data would be better displayed if the children's names are arranged in order according to distance rather than, say, alphabetically. Such children may be able to find a way of getting the program to rearrange the data.

Suggestion(s) for support
Children who find the spreadsheet too complex could use a dedicated graphing software such as Dataplot where there are only two pre-set columns and the screen display is much simpler. Provide them with plenty of paper to practise forming graphs and tables in long hand before using a computer.

Assessment opportunities

Once each child has printed a graph you will have a record of each individual's ability in handling, classifying and presenting data using IT. Sheet 104 and the their tables will provide you with evidence that the children are not reliant on the computer and that they understand the concepts and procedures necessary in making tables and graphs.

Opportunities for IT

Information technology is used here as a means to enhance the skills of handling, classifying and presenting data. If you are connected to the internet you could contact other primary schools using the World Wide Web or by e-mail and collect similar data for their school. If the school has access to digital Ordnance Survey maps and appropriate software such as Aegis, the children can measure their distance to school using the computer itself.

Display ideas

Pencil and paper versions of graphs display very effectively alongside computer generated graphs. You could get the children to draw their homes and display these alongside the graphs.

Other aspects of the Geography PoS covered

2b; 3d; 4.

Reference to photocopiable sheet

Photocopiable sheet 104 can be used to reinforce the graphing skills in a pencil and paper format. It provides a blank graph for the children to add the data for their class.

Help the children to interpret this photocopiable sheet by asking them to answer the following questions:
▲ Who lives furthest from our school?
▲ Who lives the closest?
▲ Where do most children live:
   a) up to 0.5km from the school?
   b) between 0.5km and 1.5km from the school?
   c) further than 1.5km from the school?
▲ How far from the school do you live?
▲ How far from the school does your best friend live?

Name	Distance (km)

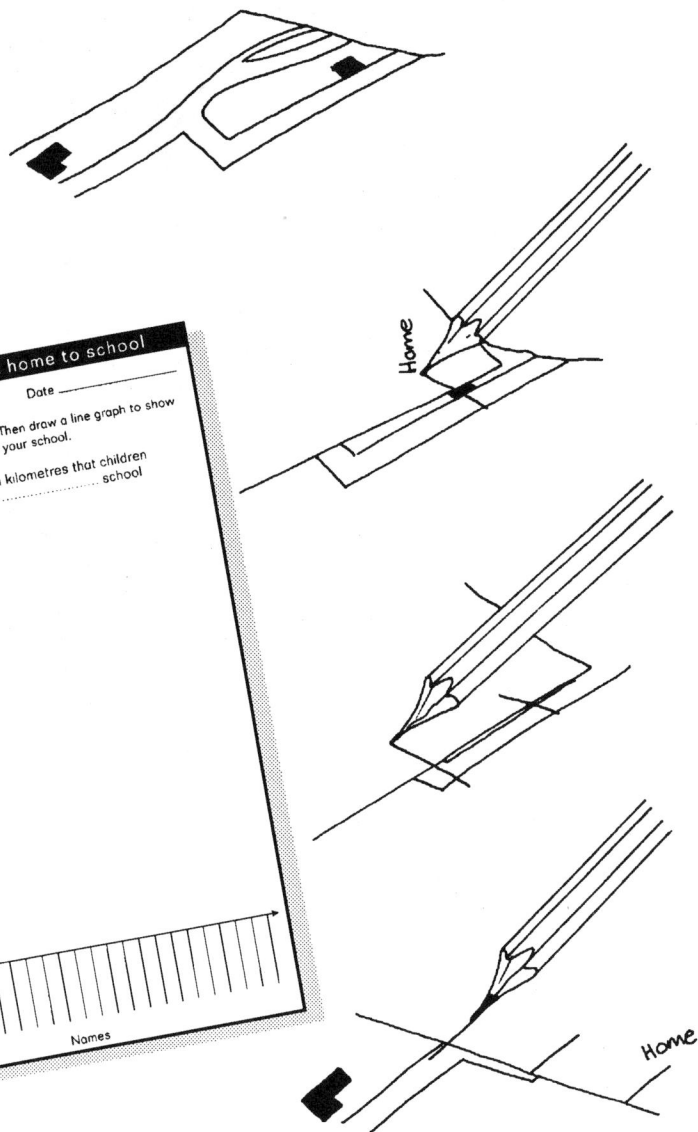

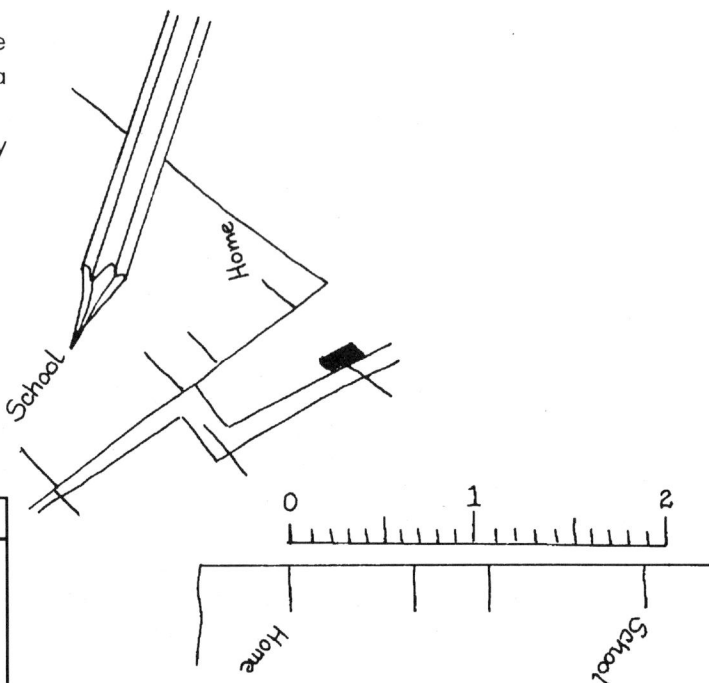

Line graph – distances from home to school

Name _____ Date _____

▲ Write in the names of children in your class. Then draw a line graph to show the distances in kilometres from their homes to your school.

Line graph showing the distances in kilometres that children in class .... live from .... school

Distance (km)

2.0 1.9 1.8 1.7 1.6 1.5 1.4 1.3 1.2 1.1 1.0 0.9 0.8 0.7 0.6 0.5 0.4 0.3 0.2 0.1

Names

0   1   2

Home   School

Mapping places

The map, from the sketch map which helps you to find a friend's house to the road atlas which helps you to navigate on a holiday, is an extremely useful tool in everyday life.

Young geographers need to acquire the skills necessary to become competent makers and users of maps. These skills include the use of plan view, scale, symbolisation and keys, grids and co-ordinates, and showing direction and distance on the map.

Children will develop in their mapping skills if these are taught in a logical progression and if the context is meaningful. Progression from large scale maps to small ones helps the children to understand. They progress from showing features pictorially, to using pictorial symbols, to using representational and then non-representational symbols. As they make this progression they will increasingly recognise the need to provide a key.

The places you choose to study with your children will provide varied opportunities with respect to mapping. Try to obtain as many real maps at different scales and of different types as you can and adapt these to the kinds of activity suggested here. The Ordnance Survey provide maps for a range of purposes and scales. Collect road atlases, local street plans, thematic maps of tourist attractions and maps showing communications networks.

The component skills of mapping can be learned though the imagined worlds of children using art work and story, and through the study of real places, peoples and themes.

SMALL, MEDIUM AND LARGE SCALE MAPS

To make plans and maps of the children's own school environment showing an appreciation of the benefits of working at different scales.

†† *Individuals.*

⊕ *10 minutes for the introduction, 20–30 minutes for the mapping activity.*

Previous skills/knowledge needed

Children should already have some experience of simple mapping, should be acquainted with the plan view and should have worked with large scale maps of places they know well. They need to have begun to learn about simple ratios in their map work.

Key background information

The same place can be mapped at different scales. The use of different scales reflects the purpose of a map. A map with a lower number (say 1:10) on the right hand side will be at a larger scale than a map with a higher number (say 1:100) on the right hand side – if the number on the left-hand side stays the same. It will contain more information about a specific place but will cover a far smaller geographical area.

Preparation

Make copies of the photocopiable sheet on page 105 for each child. A collection of different types of maps and plans at a range of scales can be used to support the activity.

Resources needed

One copy of photocopiable page 105 for each child, drawing and writing materials, examples of a range of maps for reference purpose.

Scale: ⊢±⊣⊣

What to do

Gather the children together and talk about your classroom, your school and your locality. Show the children any maps you have which cover the locality of the school and any large scale maps of the school and its grounds. An overhead projector can be used most effectively when introducing discussions about scale. (See 'Opportunities for IT'.)

Try to get the children to volunteer ideas over what the difference is between large and small scale maps. Let them appreciate that small scale maps of a place can cover a wide area but must, inevitably, include less detail and that larger scale maps will cover smaller areas but can include fine detail.

The children will enjoy coming up to the front and deciding whether various maps are large or small scale, or if you have gathered several different maps, attempting to place them in order by scale. You could refer to the ratio scale numbers on the map covers (for example, 1:50 000; 1:25 000).

Provide each child with a copy of photocopiable page 105. Explain that in box 1 they must draw as full and detailed a map of their table top as they can, that in box 2 they must draw as full and detailed a map of their classroom as they can including their table and that in box 3 they must draw as full and detailed a map of their whole school as they can including their classroom. When the children have finished, discuss which of the maps have the most detail and which covers the most area.

Suggestion(s) for extension

If you have talked to the children about the idea of ratio scales, some of the children might like to measure one centimetre on each of their maps and then measure what the same distance is on the ground for each map. Likely results might be:

▲ map of table top – 1cm:10cm
▲ map of classroom – 1cm:100cm
▲ map of school – 1cm:1000cm

Suggestion(s) for support

For children who find the scale concept a little confusing, keep emphasising that each map should fill the available box space as fully as possible. Encourage these children to take their time and put as much detail as possible into the maps.

Assessment opportunities

Completed photocopiable sheets can form a focus for discussion with each child to see whether they have recognised that increasing scale means a wider area of map coverage but a lessening degree of detail.

Opportunities for IT

The concept of scale can be reinforced with the use of an overhead projector. Project a simple map on to a white surface which has a scale line drawn on and then show the children what happens as you move the projector nearer and further away from the surface.

Display ideas

To reinforce the idea of scale choose three maps at different scales (for example, 1:10 000, 1:25 000 and 1:50 000) of the area you are studying and fold them so that the same paper area of each is displayed. Add explanatory labels saying which map shows the largest area and which shows the greatest detail.

Other aspects of the Geography PoS covered

1a; 4.

Reference to photocopiable sheet

Using photocopiable page 105, children draw maps of their table top, classroom and school in the boxes provided. The activity reinforces the concept of scale.

Three maps

Date ———

Name ———

My table top · · · · · · · · · · ·
Draw a close up view of your table top to fill this box. Add as much detail as you can. It is a **large scale** map. A large scale map shows more details.

1

My classroom · · · · · · · · · ·
Imagine that you are looking down at your classroom from the ceiling. Draw what you would see in this box. You are further away than when you drew your table so you can see more objects but not so many fine details. It will be a **medium scale** map.

2

My school · · · · · · · · ·
Imagine that you were floating over the school in a hot air balloon. What would you see? Draw it here. This will be a **small scale** map. It covers a large area but does not show fine details.

3

DIFFERENT SCALE MAPS

To use and interpret maps at a variety of scales.

†† *Individuals.*

🕐 *10 minutes for the discussion; 20 minutes for map interpretation.*

Previous skills/knowledge needed

Children will need to be acquainted with what a map is and should have some experience of drawing maps.

Key background information

When a car driver is driving between two towns it may be that a 1:50 000 (Landranger) Ordnance Survey map is more appropriate than a 1:25 000 (Pathfinder) map. This is because the first map covers a larger area. The driver would need four times as many sheets of the 1:25 000 map to cover the same area on the ground. With the first map, 1cm on the map represents 50 000cm (or 0.5km) on the ground, while on the second map, 1cm represents 25 000cm (or 0.25km) on the ground. We can see, therefore, that the larger the number on the right hand side of the ratio, the *larger* the mapped area covered on the same size piece of paper but the *less* detail mapped about each place.

Preparation

Collect a range of maps of different scales covering the same locality. You will need at least three maps of different scales which include the same real world location. Photocopy sheet 106 for each child and collect some rough paper and drawing materials.

Resources needed

A varied selection of maps with at least three different scales covering the same place, a copy of photocopiable page 106 for each child, a stock of rough paper and drawing materials.

What to do

The children should have an opportunity to examine the three maps and to identify a feature of their choice on the smallest scale of these maps.

Give each child a piece of rough paper and tell the children to draw and then cut out a square with dimensions 8cm × 8cm. It is important that the children cut the square out cleanly, leaving a frame. The frame will be used as a 'viewing window': each child uses this frame to surround one feature on the smaller scale of the three maps. Using their copy of photocopiable page 106 each child now copies the detail from the map into the first of the boxes.

The process is then repeated using the same feature as the centre point, copying the medium scale map in to the second box and the largest scale map in to the third box. Each child will end up with three 8cm × 8cm square copies from different scaled maps, all centred on the same feature.

Mapping places

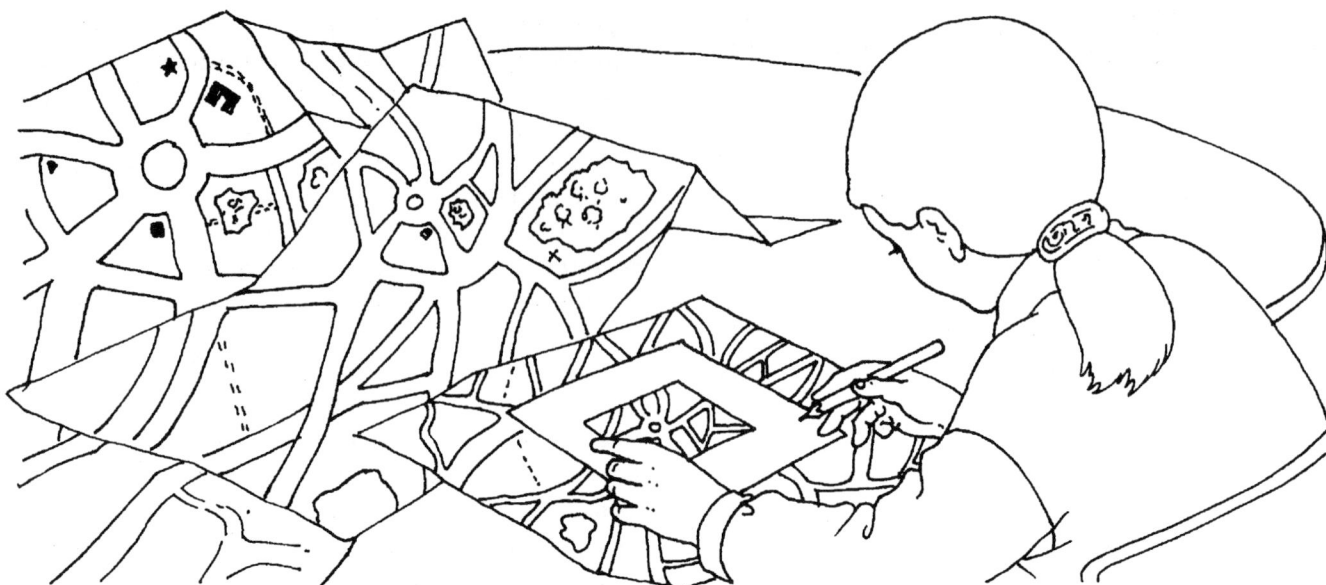

The children now prove that they understand the relationships between scale, area and detail by selecting sentences from the bottom of the photocopiable sheet and writing them beside the map squares they relate to.

When working on different maps scales it is worth considering arranging for a map-making expert, for example, from the *Ordnance Survey*, to come in to talk to the class about how modern maps are made.

Suggestion(s) for extension

More able children could list the details shown in each of the maps on a separate sheet. Children should find that there is more local detail on the large scale map.

Suggestion(s) for support

If copying within the 8cm × 8cm squares is too difficult for children, provide them with photocopied squares from the maps and ask them to assign the correct photocopied square to the correct box on photocopiable page 106.

Assessment opportunities

If children have carried out this activity individually you could use their completed photocopiable sheets to assess their ability at gleaning information from maps of different scales.

Opportunities for IT

Most Local Education Authorities hold a licence for digital versions of Ordnance Survey maps which can be used on classroom computers. There is a growing number of mapping packages available for the full range of modern computers; these allow maps to be manipulated, re-scaled, printed and even to be used as the basis for the other mapping activities undertaken on screen. IT plays an increasingly important role in map production (for example, vertical air photography and satellite imagery) and supply (for example, computer drawn and stored mapping). You may be able to give the children experience of working on a computer mapping package.

Display ideas

Using the original maps, display the three different scales of map alongside each other. Select one feature which is on all three maps and place a box the same size around the feature on each map. Children will be able to see the differences in detail and coverage area.

Other aspects of the Geography PoS covered

1a,d; 3a; 4.

Reference to photocopiable sheet

The photocopiable sheet on page 106 has three boxes of 8cm × 8cm in which children draw sections of three maps of different scales as described in the activity above. The drawing activity allows children to demonstrate their ability at working with maps of varying scale.

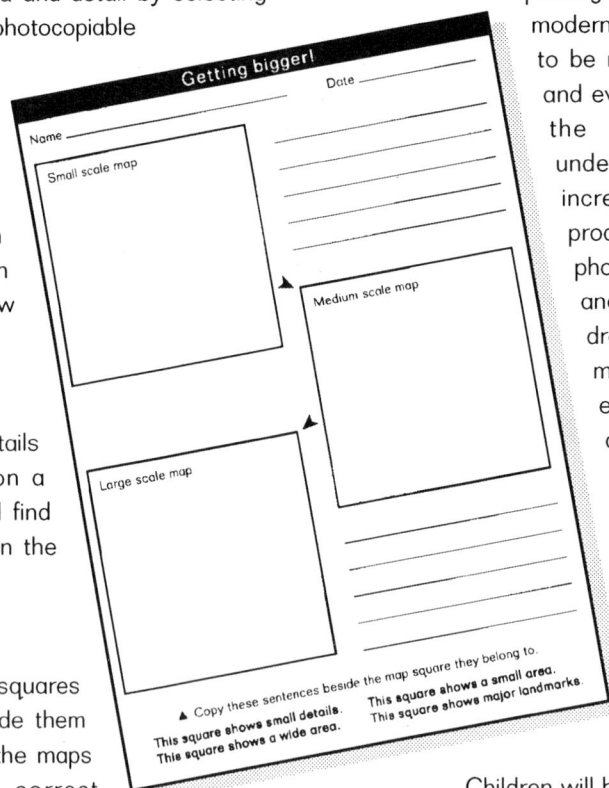

MAPPING THE SCHOOL

To make a map of the school and to remap it at a different scale.

†† Individuals working within a group.

🕐 15 minutes for an introductory walk around school; 15 minutes in the classroom for the mapping activity; 5 minutes discussion; 15 minutes in the classroom for the follow-up mapping activity.

Previous skills/knowledge needed

Children should have had experience of experimenting with simple mapping and they should be becoming increasingly aware of the purpose of maps. They should be aware of the plan view, particularly in the context of looking down on real items in the classroom.

Key background information

Scale can be thought of as the size at which we reproduce the original version of something. 'Scaling up', therefore, is making the reproduction larger than the original and 'scaling down' making it smaller. It is important that children begin to understand that as we scale down we need to include less and less detail but that we can cover a larger area of the original.

Preparation

You will need sheets of 1cm² and 2cm² A4 paper for each child. Decide on a part of your school building(s) which is appropriate for the children to map. The building(s) should, ideally, be ones around which the children can easily walk.

Resources needed

Sheets of rough paper, 1cm² and 2cm² A4 paper for each child, drawing utensils, clipboards, a copy of photocopiable pages 107 and 108 for each child.

What to do

Provide the children with copies of photocopiable page 107 'Scaling down' and ask them to complete the activity. Discuss what scaling down means.

Talk to the children about the buildings that you are going to ask them to map. Either take the children on a walk around the interior and the exterior of the buildings yourself or allow children in pairs or threes to explore the buildings themselves.

This done, give the children a 2cm² piece of paper and ask them to map the building(s) by drawing the interior and exterior walls along the lines already on the paper. The children will need support with this and may wish to do some drafting and redrafting on blank paper before moving on to the squared paper. Some children may wish to go as far as measuring the walls by pacing, using metre sticks or tape measures (see 'Suggestion(s) for extension').

Once the children have completed their 2cm² plans it is a good idea to ask them to colour them in (possibly according to a colour key) and to share results around the group or class.

Now talk to the children about why we might want to scale a map up or down. We might, for example:
▲ scale a map up to fit in more specific detail about an actual place;
▲ scale a map down to cover a wider area than would otherwise be possible on the size of paper.

The children now take their 1cm² paper and copy the map they drew on the 2cm² paper square by square. See if the children can tell you by how much the second map is smaller than the first (quarter the size by area and half the size in length). If you have used 1cm² and 2cm² paper, both at A4 in size, the children will easily be able to see that on the 1cm² paper (the smaller scale map) there is now room to map the area around the school as well.

Suggestion(s) for extension

Children could easily add more detail than has been suggested here. Doorways, the hall stage, large PE equipment and other permanent features could be added. Children could also use symbols and keys if they are ready to do so. Some children might be encouraged to measure the places they are mapping to help them make their maps accurate.

The photocopiable sheet on page 108, 'Scaling up', can be used by children capable of scaling up as well as down.

Suggestion(s) for support

Children who find this activity demanding could first carry out the same process by mapping their table area in the classroom or their classroom as a whole. If children are approaching readiness to map a large building give them as much time to walk around it as is possible.

GEOGRAPHY
KS2: PLACES

Scaling down

▲ Redraw this map of a school on to the grid below. Use one small square for each of the big squares.

You should have enough room to design the school grounds around your new, smaller scale map of the school.

If the floors of classrooms being mapped have floor tiles, the children could make use of this fact in their planning work.

Assessment opportunities

The completed copies of the maps will allow you to evaluate the children's ability at mapping the school. Look for how well they have represented shapes and spatial relationships. Compare the two squared paper maps to see how accurately the children have scaled down.

Opportunities for IT

The children could be shown how to draw a map using a drawing program and then how to scale their map up or down using percentage scaling commands. You could challenge them to map the school and then to produce scale copies at 50 per cent and 200 per cent. To make the drawing easier the background grid should be turned on and set to match the squared paper being used. If the 'snap to grid' is also activated this will help children to draw accurate vertical and horizontal lines more easily. Children should be encouraged to discuss and compare the drawing and re-scaling of the maps by computer and by hand.

Display ideas

Completed maps will make an informative display. If possible incorporate a 'real' map of the school with the children's pictures of the school. Base the display around the idea of scaling up and down. You could include children's writing explaining how they scaled their maps down.

Other aspects of the Geography PoS covered
3b; 4.

Reference to photocopiable sheets

The photocopiable sheet on page 107, 'Scaling down', provides the child with a map of a school on a 2cm² squared grid and an empty 1cm² grid on which to redraw the school. The photocopiable sheet on page 108, 'Scaling up', provides the same activity in reverse.

SYMBOLS AND KEYS

To add symbols to a map following field sketching in the school locality.

†† *Small groups.*

🕐 *30–40 minutes for a walk and field sketching in school locality; 25 minutes for the classroom mapping activity.*

Previous skills/knowledge needed

Previous work on signposts and signs in the local area will prove useful. The children will build on any early experience they may have had of field sketching, while on a walk in the locality of the school.

Key background information

When we represent something in the form of a map it becomes difficult to show detail without using symbols. This problem becomes even greater as the scale of the map gets smaller. Symbols can be representational (such as the aeroplane sign often used for airports) or non-representational (such as the red circle which depicts a railway station on an Ordnance Survey map). Once symbols begin to become non-representational, it is important that a key is used to explain their meaning.

© Crown copyright

Mapping places

© Crown copyright

Preparation

Make the necessary preparations for taking children on a short walk around the school's locality. Decide on a route which will take you past a range of different types of sign and symbol (road signs, signs on shops, hydrants, drain covers and so on). Prepare drawing paper, a clipboard for children to press on to when field sketching and copies of a large scale map of the locality.

Resources needed

Copies of a large scale map of the area you are going to walk around, field sketching equipment (paper, clipboards or an alternative, pencils), coloured pencils, a copy of photocopiable pages 109 and 110 for each child, to be used in conjunction with the activity.

What to do

Having planned a suitable route for the activity and mustered sufficient adults to accompany the children, talk to the children about what to look out for on the walk. Take them in small groups so that when a group observes a sign or symbol in the environment it is easy to stop for an individual group member to sketch the sign. Children should look out for and then sketch and label as wide a variety of symbols and signs as possible: large or small, on the ground, on posts, on street furniture or on buildings. Point out that it is only worth recording signs on immovable objects since, in the second part of the exercise, the children will be redrawing the signs on a map. Children will need to use photocopiable page 109, 'Symbols in our area', to record with each picture detailed information about where the sign is to be found.

On return to the classroom the children plot the signs and symbols they have recorded on to their copy of the map, putting them in the correct places. They will enjoy using colour to make the symbols stand out.

Finally, talk to the children about the need to make a key and help them to do this. Photocopiable page 110 could be used to develop this discussion. The key and the completed map should be mounted on to backing paper to make a complete display item.

The second column on photocopiable page 109 can be used to record information while on the walk. The third column may be filled in either on the walk or it can be used to consolidate learning in a follow-up session.

Suggestion(s) for extension

More able children will be able to differentiate between colour coding (for example, the difference between a yellow line and a white line on a road), representational symbols (for example, a 'no-cycling' sign) and non-representational symbols (for example, corporate symbols as used by companies such as banks).

Suggestion(s) for support

It is worth considering that some children may find it difficult to redraw their symbols on to their maps. Prior to taking the children on the walk, you could decide on the sketching points and number the locations on the map and on the photocopiable sheet before making the children's copies.

Assessment opportunities

Completed maps will provide you with evidence that the children understand what symbols are, can plot them in the correct place on a map and understand the reason and necessity for a key.

Opportunities for IT

The children could use an art or drawing program to create their own symbols. Once the symbols have been created they should be saved to disk. The more common symbols can be duplicated using cut and paste commands and the whole set printed, cut out and stuck on to the map. Once this has been done the children can retrieve the original symbols file and arrange them to make a key, using the text facilities of the drawing package to write and format the symbols descriptors.

Display ideas

Display the symbols copied by the children from their locality walk, alongside their completed maps and keys, and any photographs you might have of signs and symbols in the locality.

Other aspects of the Geography PoS covered

2b; 3b; 4.

Reference to photocopiable sheets

The photocopiable sheet on page 109, 'Symbols in our area', can be used either on the walk or to help structure children's work. Each child draws the symbols they observe in the first column, writes down where they observed them in the second and writes what they think the symbols mean in the third. The photocopiable sheet on page 110, 'More symbols' can be used to consolidate learning. Each child either draws a symbol to fit a description or writes a description to fit a symbol.

USING CO-ORDINATES ON MAPS

To understand the eastings (or left to right scale) before northings (or bottom to top scale) convention in the use of co-ordinates.

†† *Groups.*

🕐 *15 minutes for the discussion; 20–30 minutes for the map-based group game.*

Previous skills/knowledge needed

Children should already be acquainted with simple large scale maps and should be used to large scale plan views of the place under study (this may be your own school).

Key background information

There are several different ways to locate a specific place accurately on a map. One way is to break the map up into small areas with each area uniquely labelled (as with postcode maps). The most effective way is to superimpose a grid over the map and to provide each square in that grid with a unique reference. Doing this enables us to use co-ordinates. The bottom (and/or top) of the grid is labelled from left to right with numbers (or letters). These are referred to as 'eastings' because on a north-aligned map they run from west towards east. The left (and/or right) hand side of the grid is labelled from bottom to top with numbers (or letters). These are referred to as 'northings' because on a north-aligned map they run from south towards north. If you are using numbers as your only type of labelling (not numbers on one axis and letters on the other) then it becomes very important to use a convention as to which axis is referred to first in any grid reference. This convention is the use of 'eastings before northings'.

Preparation

Make a large, simple plan of the place you are studying. Superimpose a simple grid of 5 × 8 squares. Do this by photocopying the map and the grid on to acetate sheets and then putting both these sheets on to a photocopier. The map with its grid needs to be displayed where the whole group can easily see it.

Resources needed

Your large paper, card or projected map with its 5 × 8 grid superimposed.

What to do

Gather the children around so that everyone can see the displayed map. Talk with the children about the area the map shows. This activity is a very effective way of acquainting children with the mapped form of an area being studied and in improving their map interpretation skills.

Explain that when referring to an individual square on the grid, the children should go along the numbers at the bottom which label the columns and then up the numbers at the side which label the rows.

One child at a time comes to the front and chooses one of the squares on the grid, writing down the co-ordinates so that the rest of the group cannot see. The rest of the group then take it in turns to guess which square has been chosen by saying the co-ordinates of a square and describing what is in that square. Children try to remember which squares have been chosen until eventually someone chooses the correct square. The successful child has the next go at the front.

Observe the children carefully to ensure that they are using the correct 'along the columns then up the rows' convention and that the co-ordinates they give match the descriptions of what the map shows in the square.

Suggestion(s) for extension

For able children to demonstrate that they are in fact using the co-ordinate system to assist their interpretation of a map, you could ask the child at the front to give a description of the square chosen using information on the map. Good map users will be able to identify the correct square almost immediately.

Suggestion(s) for support

Some children may like to play the game in pairs with one of the children writing down the co-ordinates of squares as they are picked to ensure that they do not waste their go on a square already tried by someone else. Copies of photocopiable page 111 can be used to record which squares have already been picked.

Assessment opportunities

Sit with individuals and check that they are describing the squares correctly that they are giving co-ordinates for, and that they are using the correct 'eastings then northings' convention.

Opportunities for IT

Children can draw their own maps with grids on to acetate sheet and show them to the rest of the group to play one of the varieties of this game using the overhead projector.

Display ideas

Involve some of the children in making a large wall display map with a grid. Label the map with questions where the answers are unique grid locations (for example 'Where is the...?'). Provide the answers under flaps for users of this interactive display to check that they have identified the correct squares.

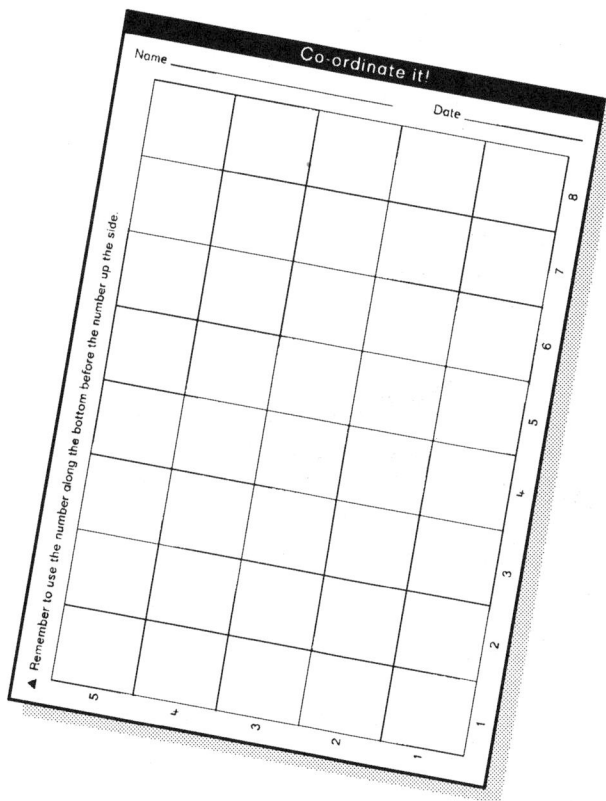

Other aspects of the Geography PoS covered

2c; 3e; 4.

Reference to photocopiable sheet

The photocopiable sheet on page 111 can be used in support of this activity with each child marking off those squares in the 5 x 8 grid which have been eliminated by being incorrectly picked. If children write the initials of the child at the front as small as they can in each square eliminated, the photocopiable sheet can be used for several goes.

USING FOUR-FIGURE GRID REFERENCES

To develop an understanding of the four-figure grid reference system.

†† *Individuals.*

🕐 *15 minutes for the discussion; 20 minutes to fill in the photocopiable sheet and do the map activity.*

Previous skills/knowledge needed

Children should have had some experience of using simple co-ordinates and should have been introduced to the 'eastings then northings' convention.

Key background information

Once introduced to the idea of uniquely locating mapped details using co-ordinates on a grid, children should be introduced to the four-figure grid reference system. This system is used by the Ordnance Survey to break up the national mapping grid into regions of 100km x 100km (a square made of 10 000 kilometre squares). For the national grid referencing system to work, each unique square within a 100km x 100km area must have two numbers in its column and row labels. These numbers are located on the lines to the left and bottom of each square and range from 00 to 99.

Preparation

Obtain a 1:25 000 (Pathfinder) Ordnance Survey map covering the area you are studying. Display it so that one of the 10km x 10km squares is available to the children. Decide on ten major features on the map and write the name of each one against one of the letters A to J on a copy of photocopiable page 112. Then photocopy the amended sheet for each child.

Resources needed

A displayed 10km x 10km portion of the 1:25 000 map of the area you are studying, a copy of the amended photocopiable pages 112 and 113 for each child, pencils.

What to do

Four-figure grid-referencing can be introduced by using photocopiable page 113. Some children may benefit from completing this sheet before the main part of the activity. Show the children the map and explain to them that there are 100 squares on the map, each one labelled with two numbers on its left side along the bottom of the map and two numbers on its lower side on the left hand side of the map. It is a good idea to reinforce this by drawing a diagram on the board as follows:

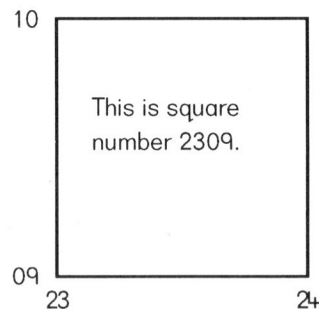

10

This is square number 2309.

09

23   24

Give each child a copy of the amended photocopiable sheet on page 112. Tell the children that they are to find each of the places A to J on the map and that they are then to work out the four-figure grid reference for each place and write the reference in the appropriate column on the sheet.

The learning is reinforced using the top part of the photocopiable sheet. The children copy the numbers from the 1:25 000 map into the relevant boxes along the bottom and left hand side of the 10 x 10 grid remembering to put the numbers against the lines, not the squares. Lastly they can write the letters A to J in the correct places on this grid.

Make the display interactive by labelling it with questions relating to features in specific grid squares where the answers are four-figure grid references. The answers could be hidden under 'lift-the-flap' features within the display.

Other aspects of the Geography PoS covered

1d; 4.

Reference to photocopiable sheets

Photocopiable page 112 is used for children to record which grid squares certain mapped features are in as described in 'What to do'. Photocopiable page 113 can be used to introduce the activity or to support the children needing help with reading four-figure grid references.

Suggestion(s) for extension

Children who have a good understanding of the operation of four-figure grid references could use the copy of the 1:25 000 map to set each other imaginary routes within the square being studied. They could make written descriptions of their routes using four-figure grid-referencing.

Suggestion(s) for support

The photocopiable sheet on page 113 can be used to support children who are having some trouble with understanding the system. The children fill in the grid references for nine items marked on a simple 3 × 3 grid.

Assessment opportunities

The photocopiable sheets on pages 112 and 113 will provide evidence of individual children's ability at operating the four-figure grid referencing system.

Opportunities for IT

Set up a simple map as an overlay for a concept keyboard, ensuring that the grid on the map exactly matches the grid formed by the individual cells on the concept keyboard. Give the grid four-figure grid labelling along the bottom and left side of the overlay. This then can be linked to an overlay program to involve the children in using the grid.

Further reinforcement could be given using specific geographical software which gives children more practice in writing and identifying co-ordinates using simple maps shown on the computer screen.

Display ideas

Make a mapping display centred around the 1:25 000 maps for your own locality and/or other contrasting UK localities.

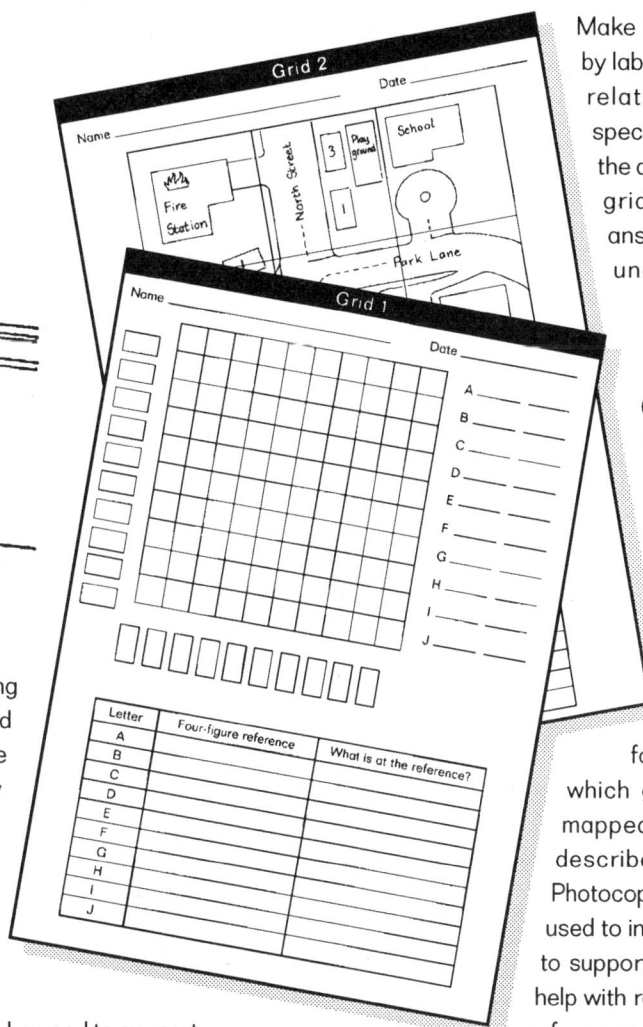

NORTH, EAST, SOUTH, WEST

To understand the purpose of the four points of the compass.

†† Groups.

🕐 15 minutes for the discussion; 20 minutes or more for the group activity.

Previous skills/knowledge needed

This activity can be used to prepare children for using compass directions in the context of the localities studied during the Key Stage but needs little in the way of prerequisite knowledge or skills.

Key background information

A compass is an instrument which indicates direction and which can, therefore, help us to navigate our way across space. Children are most likely to use compasses later in their school careers to help them on walking expeditions but in adult life compasses are used by a wide range of people including sailors, aeroplane pilots, surveyors and rally car drivers.

Preparation

Collect a globe, a map of your region and at least one compass. You will need to write the words north, east, south and west, each on the top of a large piece of card. Consider how, as part of the lesson, you will fasten each of these pieces of card on the wall at the northerly, easterly, southerly and westerly extremities of the room.

Resources needed

A globe and at least one compass, a map of your region, four large pieces of card, Blu-Tack, marker pens, copies of photocopiable pages 114 and 115 for each child if required.

What to do

Show the children the globe and ask individuals to show the rest of the group the location of our country and any other localities being studied. Encourage children to share their knowledge of where the north pole and the south pole are and which way around the Earth is heading westward (to the left as you look at a normal globe) and which way is eastward (to the right as you look at a normal globe).

Use individual volunteers to hold the compass and to point to each of the four main points of the compass. Aim at all of the children recognising which way from their classroom leads eventually to the north pole.

Once the group has established each of the four directions from the centre of your classroom, ask four different children to take one of the large pieces of card to the relevant place around the classroom edge. The rest of the children look at the globe and identify places that are in each direction from where your school is. They identify more local places using a regional map and establish in which direction any contrasting localities lie. Ask some of the children to list

places to the north on the north card and other groups of children to do the same for the other compass points on large pieces of card. You will end up with four large pieces of card in appropriate positions around the edge of the classroom, each with a list of real places which are in that direction from your school.

Suggestion(s) for extension

If children have coped well with using the four main points of the compass, introduce the idea of eight points and involve them in carrying out the listing and map interpretation part of the activity using eight large pieces of card.

Suggestion(s) for support

Photocopiable sheet 114 can be used to help children. If they need support in applying the idea of compass points to the globe and the maps, mark your school's location using Blu-Tack on the globe and stickers on the maps and add arrows pointing in each of the directions.

Assessment opportunities

Photocopiable page 115 can be used to assess children's understanding of what each of the compass points mean. Observation of individuals at the group discussion part of the activity may also be useful.

Opportunities for IT

Children could use a word processing package to produce the list of places for each of the direction cards. They could try out different fonts and font sizes to make the list easy to read from anywhere in the classroom. A growing number of mapping packages are available, many on CD-ROM, which children could use to assist their research.

Display ideas

Position a small table in the centre of the classroom with a compass on it. Children will use this to check the directions

of the four (or eight) direction cards. Provide a selection of maps, atlases and books about places on this table so that children can research more places to add to the lists on the walls.

Other aspects of the Geography PoS covered

1a, b, d; 3a, e; 4.

Reference to photocopiable sheets

Photocopiable page 114 can be used to support the children's gathering of mapped information as part of this activity. Children record places which are to the north, east, south and west and are local, in their country and further afield, using the boxes on the sheet. Photocopiable page 115 can be used to assess or extend the children's understanding.

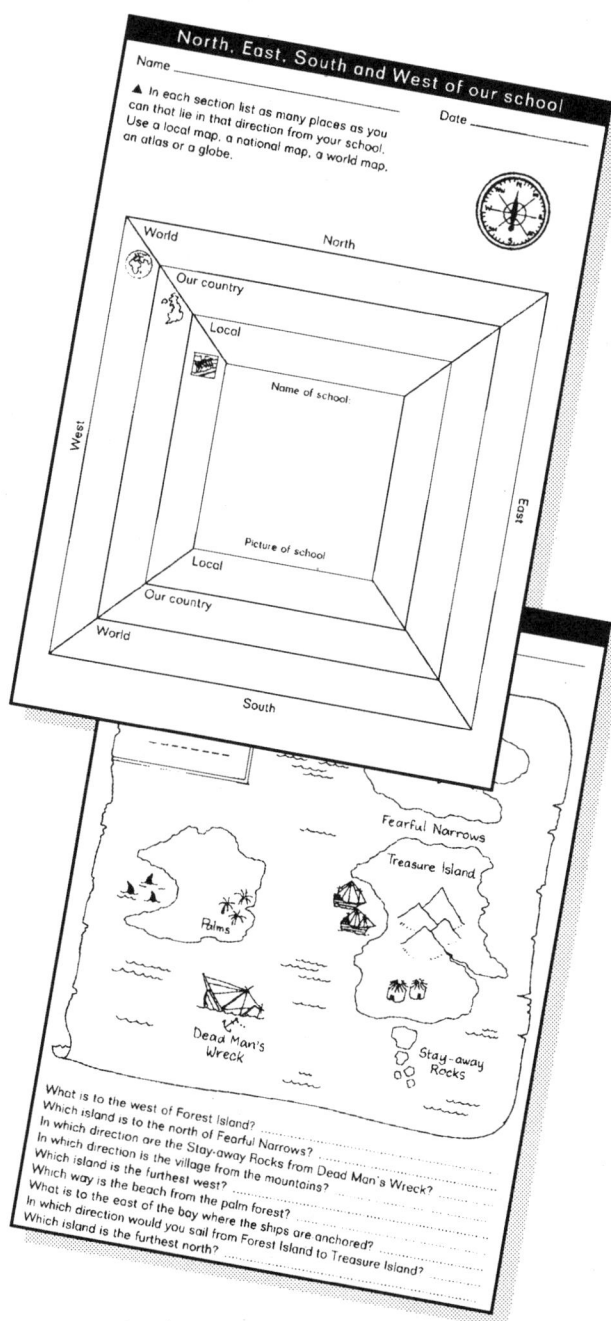

North, East, South and West of our school

What is to the west of Forest Island?
Which island is to the north of Fearful Narrows?
In which direction are the Stay-away Rocks from Dead Man's Wreck?
In which direction is the village from the mountains?
Which island is the furthest west?
Which way is the beach from the palm forest?
What is to the east of the bay where the ships are anchored?
In which direction would you sail from Forest Island to Treasure Island?
Which island is the furthest north?

WHICH WAY IS IT?

To be able to measure direction using the four points of the compass.

†† *Pairs within a group.*

🕐 *10 minutes for the group discussion; 25 minutes for the map activity in pairs.*

Previous skills/knowledge needed

Children should have been introduced to the locality you are studying and should be beginning to recognise it on the maps you have. Some directional knowledge and vocabulary might already be in place, for example, left and right.

Key background information

We can use localities being studied to help teach direction. Once children understand concepts like 'left', 'right', 'in front' and 'behind' they should be helped to understand north, east, south and west. The key concepts here are that north is always north and that north, east, south and west always go around the compass rose in a clockwise direction with ninety degrees (or a right angle) between them.

Preparation

Obtain a globe and make photocopies of a section of a large scale map of the locality adding a north, east, south, west compass rose. (Ensure that your school has the appropriate LEA photocopying licence to do this.) You might choose to make copies of photocopiable page 116 to support children in the activity. You will also find a national map of the locality's country useful.

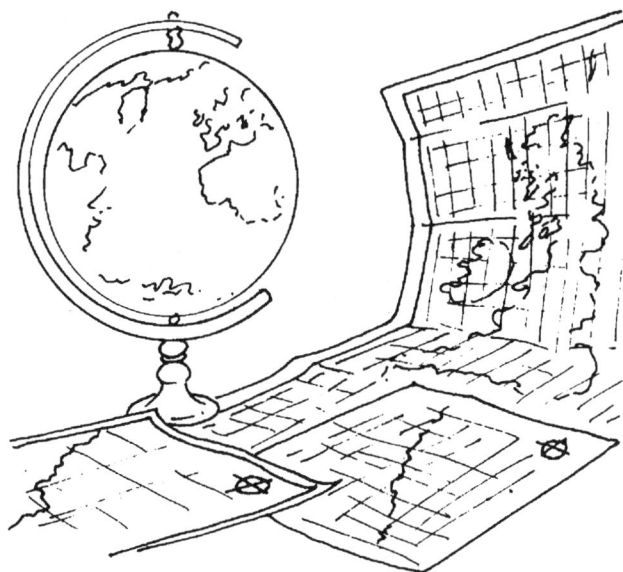

Resources needed

Globe, national map and one photocopy for each pair of the large scale map of the locality being studied including a compass rose, A4 photocopies of the large scale map showing the relevant locality.

**GEOGRAPHY
KS2: PLACES**

What to do

Talk to the children about what they understand north, east, south and west to mean. They may refer to Santa Claus, the north pole, reindeer, and polar bears when talking about 'north'.

Use the globe and a compass. Establish that wherever you are on the Earth's surface, north is always towards the north pole across the curved surface of the Earth. Get children to take it in turns to stand in different parts of the classroom and use the compass to show which way the north pole is.

Get the children to locate on the globe the country which contains the locality being studied. Use the national map as reference to help the children to recognise the country's outline and to help them put the actual locality in context. The children will discover which way is north in the locality itself.

Put the children into pairs and explain that each member of a pair will set a route from a starting point to an eventual destination using any routeways on the photocopied map. The first child writes out the route using only the words north, east, south, west to describe direction but adding any other description which will aid the other child to follow the route. Encourage children to use terms like 'ahead', 'turn', 'next', 'next but one', 'before', 'after', 'along' and 'opposite'. Photocopiable page 116 can be used to provide a word or phrase bank which the children might find helpful.

Once each child has devised their route they challenge their partner to follow it on the map.

Suggestion(s) for extension

If children are already capable of using the main eight points of the compass then they could be paired accordingly and allowed to go to this further stage.

Suggestion(s) for support

If children are going to have difficulty understanding which lines on the maps are which, you could bolden routeways before photocopying.

Assessment opportunities

Gauge the degree to which children are successful at measuring direction by asking individuals to take you through their route verbally. This could be done as a part of a group reporting back session.

Opportunities for IT

The children could use a ROAMER or other floor robot and direct it around a course of obstacles. Alternatively, a large floor map of an imaginary place, such as an island, could be created with different features on it. Children could guide ROAMER around this map using directions involving north, east, south and west. Although they can phrase their instructions using compass directions they will need to interpret these into ROAMER commands which deal in right and left turns (for example, if the ROAMER is facing east a turn to the north will need to be phrased as a left turn). A similar activity could be undertaken using screen turtle graphics.

Display ideas

Make a large compass using a backing card with the four points on and a large pointer. Fasten the compass point so that it stands proud of a table top but leave the card with the

Which way word bank

Name			Date	
		east	west	
north	south	left	right	
up	down	in front	behind	
before	after	next but one	opposite	
ahead	next	turn	fork	
along	alongside	go	out of	
branch	into	far	distant	
near	close	until	beside	
over	across	narrow	stop	
move	wide	forwards	backwards	
long	short			

four points on so that it can be rotated. Children will enjoy lining up the 'N' or 'North' with the point of the compass pointer thus reinforcing the fact that north is always north.

Other aspects of the Geography PoS covered
3a; 4; 5a.

Reference to photocopiable sheets
The photocopiable page 116 provides a bank of words and phrases which might support children as they write their instructions for their partner to follow. The sheet can be used as a spelling word bank. You could protect this sheet with transparent adhesive and cut out the cards if your children are using a word bank.

MEASURING DISTANCE

To be able to measure distance using a map with a scale.

†† *Individuals within group.*

🕐 *20 minutes for the introduction; 25 minutes for the activity on the photocopiable sheet.*

Previous skills/knowledge needed
Children should have been introduced to the locality you are studying and should have had some experience of using maps, and some understanding of scale.

Key background information
Maps have a number of uses. One is the measurement of distance between places without having to actually go to the place with a tape measure. Every map should include somewhere a ratio scale (for example, 1:25 000) and a linear scale which actually shows what a unit of distance on the ground looks like on the map.

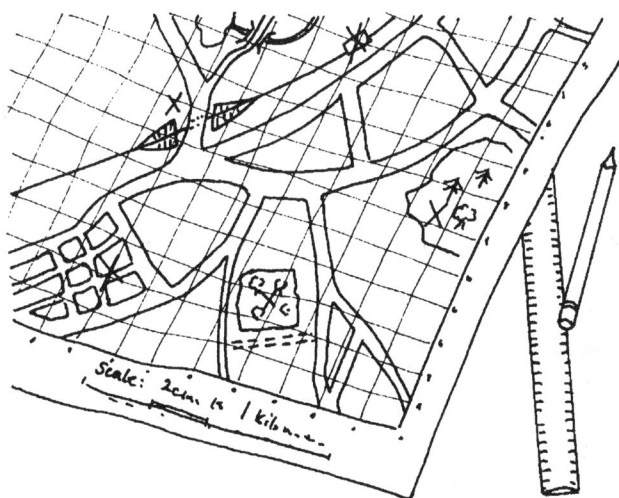

Preparation
Photocopy an A4 section of a map of the area you are studying which includes a number of clearly identifiable features. (Ensure that your school has a suitable LEA photocopy licence.) Mark 11 features on the photocopy with crosses, ten of them surrounding the eleventh which should be fairly central. Make copies of the map (with its 11 crosses) and copies of photocopiable page 117 for each child. Ensure that the map includes the linear scale from the bottom of the master map (this may have to be photocopied, trimmed and stuck on the bottom of the photocopied map before the final photocopying). Prepare strips of straight-edged paper.

Resources needed
Copies of the map with its 11 crosses and copies of photocopiable page 117 for each child, the original map which you copied for discussion purposes, strips of scrap paper cut with straight edges, pencils.

What to do

Show the children the map which you have used to photocopy your map sheets. Ask individuals to come to the front and to identify the 11 features. As children identify each feature, ask them to mark it so that you can all remember it. (This could be done with small lumps of Blu-Tack.)

Ask the children to volunteer guesses about the distances (in metres or kilometres, depending on what scale you are working at) between the central point and the other points.

Show the children how to measure distance on a map using a strip of paper, marking the start and finish point on the paper, and then transferring down to the linear scale.

Show the children the photocopied maps with the crosses already marked and ask them to work out the distances from the central point to each of the other points. Ask them to record their results on their copies of photocopiable sheet 117.

The photocopiable sheet can be completed in two stages with the children first recording the straight line distances and then the distances by road, track or pathway.

Suggestion(s) for extension

Involve the more able children in calculating the distances by actual routeways. They will have to mark the position of bends on their strips of paper and turn the paper until it lines up with the next straight bit of routeway, effectively 'straightening-out' the distance so that it can be measured against the scale. (See the illustration on page 22 in the activity 'Spreadsheet presentation'.)

Suggestion(s) for support

You could make two different sets of map sheet, one set with more difficult routes and longer distances, and one set with straighter and shorter distances.

Assessment opportunities

Completed copies of photocopiable page 117 will help you to assess the children's ability to measure distance using a map.

Opportunities for IT

There are mapping packages available which enable children to identify two locations on a computer stored map and then ask the computer to work out the distance between the two points. Where schools have access to Ordnance Survey digital maps this can be done in the context of their own locality work.

Alternatively, children could be introduced to such packages as Auto-Route which automatically calculates the distances between places in the UK and/or Europe over several routes. The information can be displayed in a table or as a map. Children are fascinated that technology can do this for them.

Display ideas

The original map and copies of completed children's work can be displayed as a part of a general display on the locality being studied, or on measurement as a mathematical skill.

Other aspects of the Geography PoS covered
3a; 4.

Reference to photocopiable sheet
Children measure distances using the map scale on the photocopied map sheets you have prepared and transfer these distances on to photocopiable page 117. There is a column for straight line distances and one for distances by routeway.

GUIDED TOUR

To be able to use a map to set and follow a route.

†† *Groups of four.*

🕐 *5 minutes for the introduction; 15 minutes for the walk making a route; 10 minutes for the class activity; 10 minutes for the walk following a route.*

Previous skills/knowledge needed
Children should have an idea of what a guided tour is. They should have an idea of the geographical layout of their school.

Key background information
Maps can be used to help us follow routes. In this context the map truly becomes a tool which enables us to do things. A map, can, for example, provide us with a guide for a sight-seeing tour around an historic town, a sketched version can be the tool which helps us to guide a lost lorry driver. Some supermarkets provide us with maps to help us plan our routes around the products they sell. Children should become increasingly proficient both at setting routes on a map and following routes from a map which other people have devised.

Preparation
Obtain or make an A4 map of your school which includes the interior of the buildings and make enough copies for each group of four children. Make different-coloured sets of ten cards, each card in a set containing a different letter of the alphabet. You may need one copy of photocopiable page 118 per child.

Resources needed
The large scale plan of your school and the copies for each group, sets of ten small cards, each with a different letter of the alphabet, at least one copy of photocopiable page 118 per child (optional).

What to do
This activity can be introduced using photocopiable page 118. Children write a guide to the mapped route on the welcome map of an imaginary primary school. Group the children in fours and give each group time to walk around the school buildings and grounds. Tell them that they have to devise a route for showing visitors around the school.

Before they set off, ask them to list the ten key places of interest visitors might wish to see. As they walk around the school get the children to leave one of their coloured letter cards in each of the places that they would show a visitor, recording it on a table like the one below.

Letter card	Name of place
C	My classroom
G	Gymnasium

Once each group has returned, give them a copy of the school map and ask them to plot the route they have decided on. This is best done using a neat, dashed line. You can then ask the children to mark ten dots on the map relating to the ten places they identified as of most interest to visitors to the school and labelling each one with a number.

Each group can then challenge other groups to follow their routes and find the letters at each location.

Mapping places

Suggestion(s) for extension

The concept of route-making for a purpose will be further developed if you ask children capable of doing so to write out their routes to accompany their maps; rather like the written description in a guidebook.

Suggestion(s) for support

Children who find the scale of operation difficult could first of all be asked to carry out this activity within the confines of the classroom itself.

Assessment opportunities

Get groups to report back on the route they followed and on how easy it was to do so. Note whether individuals are showing the skills necessary to correctly follow a route on a map.

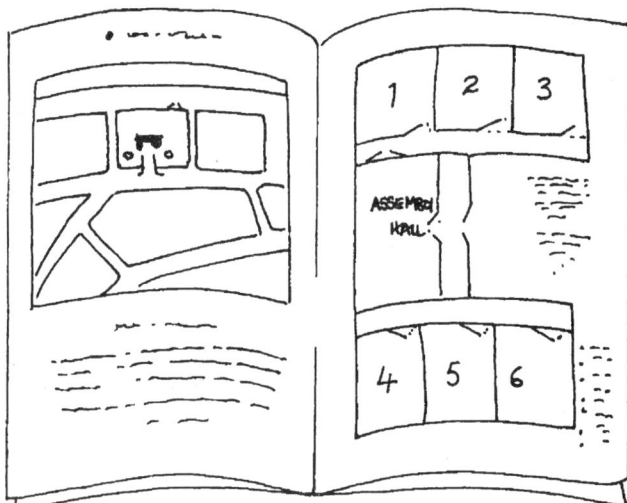

Opportunities for IT

Children could work in groups using a desktop publishing package to present a simple visitor's guide to the school, showing the route and describing what is seen at each location. This will involve them in using IT to draw the map, possibly using a drawing package or scanning their own hand drawn maps. They could add pictures scanned from their own drawings or photographs of the school, or digitised from a video camera. A good layout is the form of a three fold (sheet of A4) which gives six columns for children to work in, each one needing an illustration and some text.

A more sophisticated approach would be to use a multimedia authoring package to create an electronic presentation which links pictures, maps, text and sounds, and even moving images taken with a video camera.

Display ideas

Completed maps can be displayed very effectively, particularly if children have colour coded the places on them, along with any written 'guidebook' descriptions the children may have done.

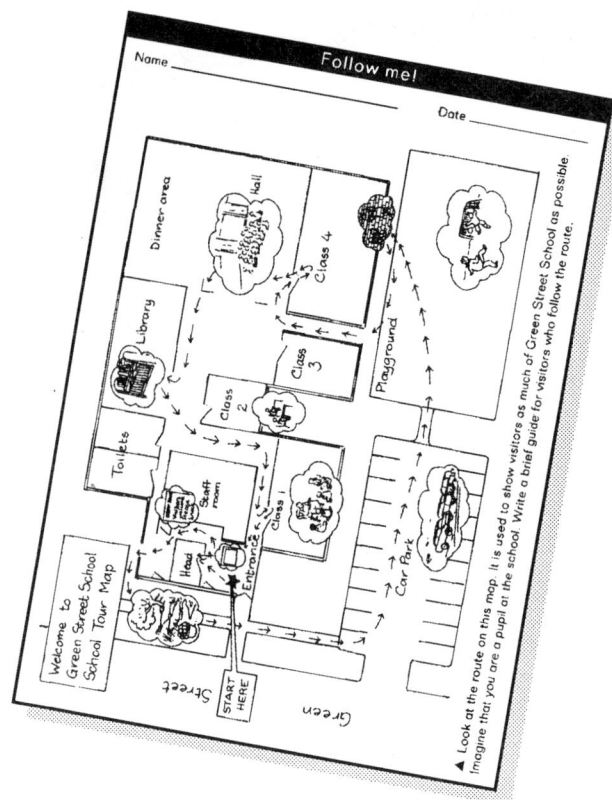

Other aspects of the Geography PoS covered

1a; 3a; 4; 5a.

Reference to photocopiable sheet

Photocopiable page 118 can be used either to introduce the activity or as a follow-up. Children look at the guided tour route on the 'Welcome to Green Street School' leaflet and then write a guide to go with the route. The sheet can be used as an example of the sort of route they will design and follow around their own school as part of the main activity.

THE WORLD IN A BOOK

To be able to use an atlas to assist with studies. To be able to use the contents and index pages of an atlas.

†† *Pairs within a group.*

🕐 *15 minutes for the group discussion; 25 minutes for paired work.*

Previous skills/knowledge needed
Children should be used to the idea of using a reference book such as a dictionary, encyclopaedia or non-fiction information book. Previous work on the seven continents will prove useful.

Key background information
The atlas is effectively a very large paper map, covering the whole world, which has been cut up into separate pages to make it manageable. The world atlas is an essential reference book for the geographer and certainly for the Key Stage 2 classroom. Children will need to refer to atlases as a part of their geographical studies but there will also be occasions when the atlas comes into its own quite unexpectedly. Children will bring information into the classroom with respect to their holidays, where their relatives live and places they have read about or seen on television.

The atlas can help children develop an appreciation of the way in which places 'nest' within each other (cities are within counties or states, which are within countries, which are within continents). It is very important that children are increasingly able to use the contents and index pages of atlases.

Preparation
Each pair will require a copy of photocopiable page 119 and you will need to gather a stock of world atlases. Prepare a

copy of a world map and a globe and position them where you and the children will be able to see them.

Resources needed
Copies of photocopiable sheet 119 for each pair, a supply of world atlases, writing materials, a copy of a world map and a globe.

What to do
Gather the children around and discuss the globe and the world map. See what the children can tell you about places in the world. Do they know that villages, towns and cities are in countries which are in continents? Can they name any of the continents?

Have a look at some of the atlases and get the idea over that an atlas is a world map which has been chopped up to fit in a book. Try some children out at finding places using the contents page and the index.

Put the children into pairs, giving each pair a copy of the photocopiable sheet. Get the children to use an atlas to help them complete their copy of photocopiable page 119. They should use the index and contents pages to help them research each of the places listed on the sheet.

Suggestion(s) for extension
Ask pairs who complete the sheet easily to make their own similar table, to copy down the six countries listed at the bottom of the photocopiable sheet and to research a feature (a river, forest or mountain) that is in each of these countries. The children could then supplement their table with other places found in their atlases.

Suggestion(s) for support
Atlases vary greatly in their complexity. For children who find using the alphabetic referencing system difficult, use a simpler atlas with larger index and label text and fewer entries. Pair the children so that a more able reader supports a less

Mapping places

Find it out

Name _____   Date _____

▲ Use your atlas to fill in the following columns.

	Country or countries this place is in	Continent this place is in	Page or pages in your atlas where you found the place
Montevideo			
River Missouri			
Ural Mountains			
Queen Maud Land			
Wellington			
River Ganges			
Atlas Mountains			
Nairobi			
River Parana			
Great Dividing Range			
London			
River Rhône			
Andes Mountains			
Karachi			
River Darling			
Rocky Mountains			
Los Angeles			
River Nile			
Athens			
Pennine Mountains			
Nepal			
Columbia			
Chad			
Austria			
Canada			
Papua New Guinea			

able reader and instruct the children that one of them should find the required page number using the index and contents pages and that the other should then find the correct page. This ensures that both have a role in the activity.

Assessment opportunities
Either use the sheets the children have completed to evaluate their understanding or sit with individuals and ask them to find a place you know to be in the index of the atlas.

Opportunities for IT
There are opportunities here for children to interrogate computer mapping packages and CD-ROM atlases and to ask the computer to search for specific places and to show their location on a world map. Similar opportunities are increasingly available on the Internet.

Display ideas
Create a display which reinforces the general idea of the whole world (represented by a world map and a globe) being sectioned up to fit into a book (represented by an atlas). Provide atlases on a table in front of the display and a list of places for children to find. Provide small pieces of card and some Blu-Tack so that once the children have used the display to find one of the places, they can write the name on a piece of the card and stick it in the right place on the wall map.

Other aspects of the Geography PoS covered
1a, d; 3a, e; 4.

Reference to photocopiable sheet
Photocopiable page 119 consists of a list of world cities, rivers and mountains and invites children to use the atlas to find the country and the continent in which these features are located. The children are asked to write down the page numbers where they found the information.

◆ KNOW YOUR COUNTRY

To have a basic knowledge of the UK and to be able to identify certain features on a UK map.

†† Individuals.

🕐 10 minutes for the discussion; 10 minutes for the map work; 20–30 minutes for story writing.

Previous skills/knowledge needed
Previous work on the UK will prove useful. Children will need to be able to write a story.

Key background information
The National Curriculum expects children to be able to identify 17 points of reference on a map of the UK (20 points if the three borders are included) by the end of Key Stage 2. A basic locational knowledge will help children to put other geographical learning in context. Here we include the three borders between England and Wales, Scotland and England, and Northern Ireland and the Republic of Ireland which are also included on Map A in the National Curriculum document. The points of reference are:
▲ the countries England, Wales and Scotland and the province of Northern Ireland;
▲ the three borders;

▲ the four capitals (London, Cardiff, Edinburgh and Belfast);

▲ the English Channel and the Irish Sea;

▲ the rivers Thames, Severn and Trent;

▲ the four upland areas of the Pennines, the Lake District, the Grampian Mountains and the Cambrian Mountains.

Preparation

Each child will require a copy of photocopiable pages 120 and 121. They may also require some additional writing paper and some paper suitable for rough work. Display a wall map of the UK for general reference purposes. It is a good idea to display place name and travelling words around the wall map.

used to help provide the children with a structure and some stimulus. They will find this much easier if you provide a bank of travelling words and place words, possibly displayed around the wall map of the UK.

Once all of the group or class have written their stories get the children to tell them to each other.

Suggestion(s) for extension

Encourage more able children to research what the route would actually be like — to use information books to research the places through which their route passes. These children could draw in detail and add place labels to the UK map on photocopiable sheet 120.

Resources needed

Copies of photocopiable pages 120 and 121, writing paper, rough paper, pencils, a wall map of the UK.

What to do

Talk to the children about the UK. This is a good opportunity to begin to get across the difference between each of the constituent countries and the fact that The British Isles contains the two nations of the United Kingdom of Great Britain and Northern Ireland, and the Republic of Ireland.

Each child is going to write a story about a character of their choice and that character's adventures as it travels around the UK. Explain to the children that they have to map a route which joins every one of the 17 places marked on photocopiable page 120 (including the box key) and which has a starting and a finishing point. Ask the children to use the wall map and/or atlases to help them to label each of the places on the map.

The map work done, each child then writes a story relating their character's adventure. Photocopiable page 121 can be

Suggestion(s) for support

For some children the written part of the activity might prove too extending. You could put these children into 'writing teams' in which each child takes responsibility for one part of a route which has been jointly decided between them.

Assessment opportunities

Photocopiable page 120 could provide a test of the children's knowledge of the 17 places marked.

Opportunities for IT

Children could use a word processor to type and present their stories of the route around the UK. A clipart map of the UK, or a scanned version of a map drawn by you, could be loaded into a drawing package and the children write and position their labels on the map. This map could be used within a word processor to help illustrate the story the children have written.

A more ambitious project would be to use a multi-media authoring package to create a class presentation of the trip around the UK. Children could work in pairs on a part of the route, selecting the places, researching information about the town or features they are visiting, using a mapping package to calculate the distance between the places and research other information from CD-ROMs, books or other guides. Once the children have gathered their information they can decide how they are going to present it perhaps using two or three screens. The title screen could be set up using a map of the UK with the places marked on it. When the user clicks on a place, they are presented with the information about that place and a route to get to the next place on the map.

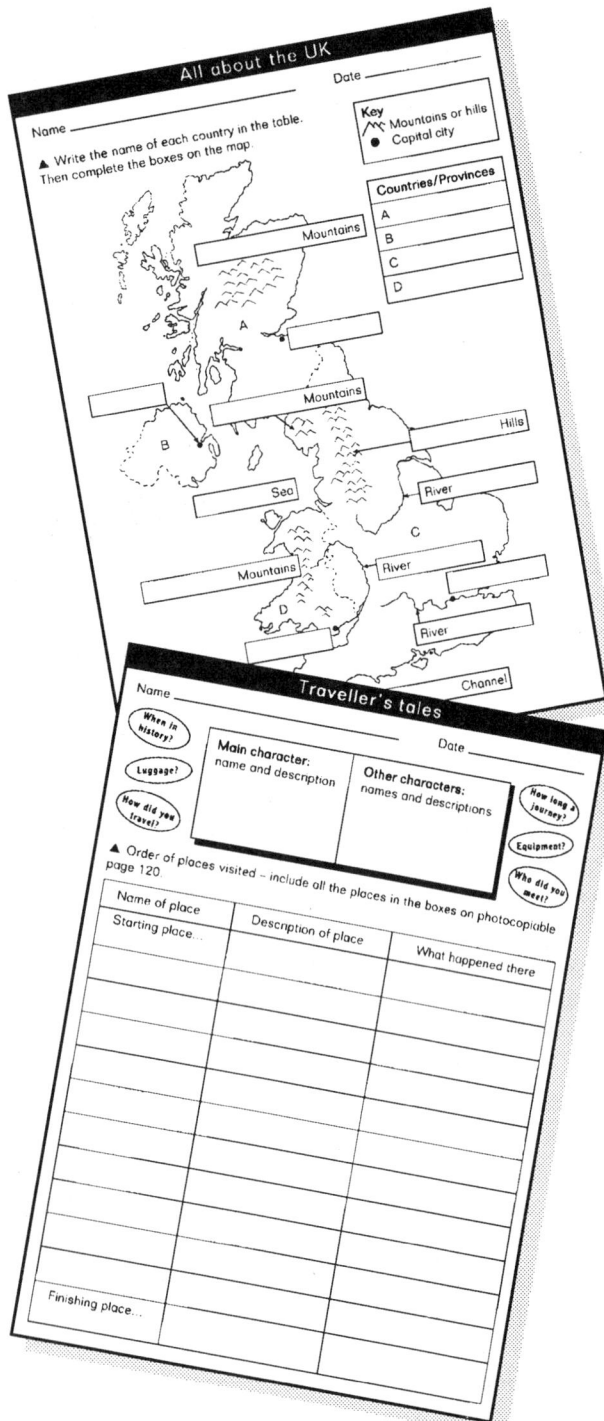

Display ideas
The wall map, the globe, the children's completed maps and stories and the wall map labels and words will all add together to make a colourful and interesting display. Make sure you display children's maps with their own stories.

Other aspects of the Geography PoS covered
1a, d; 3a, e; 4; 5a.

Reference to photocopiable sheets
Photocopiable page 120 has a map of the UK to which children add a route, labelling the 17 reference points required for Key Stage 2. This map can then be used to stimulate story writing using photocopiable page 121 aimed at reinforcing this locational knowledge.

WELCOME TO EUROPE!

To have a basic knowledge of Europe and to be able to identify certain features on a map of Europe.
†† *Individuals.*
🕐 *10 minutes for the discussion; 30 minutes for mapping and poster design.*

Previous skills/knowledge needed
Children should have some idea about what guide books are and will benefit if they have had some experience of writing to put over an argument.

Key background information
At Key Stage 2 the National Curriculum expects children to gather a certain amount of factual knowledge of Europe. Children are expected to be able to identify 16 points of reference on a European map (National Curriculum Map B) as follows:
▲ France and its capital, Paris;
▲ Germany and its capital, Berlin;
▲ the Republic of Ireland and its capital, Dublin;
▲ Italy and its capital, Rome;
▲ Spain and its capital, Madrid;
▲ the United Kingdom and its capital, London;
▲ the Mediterranean and North Sea;
▲ the River Rhine;
▲ The Alps mountain range.

In reality we might well hope that children gain an even broader locational knowledge of Europe. This minimum expectation does help us remember that a basic locational knowledge helps children put their geographical learning in context.

Preparation
Obtain and display a wall map of Europe. Have some Blu-Tack and some lengths of string ready so that you can mark

suggested routes on the wall map. Photocopy sheet 122 for each child. Copies of tourist guidebooks and travel brochures will provide a useful stimulus for this activity so, if you can, collect some of these. Collect glue and paper for making posters.

Resources needed
Europe wall map, one copy of photocopiable page 122 for each child, copies of tourist guide books and travel brochures, Blu-Tack and lengths of string, poster design paper (for example, A3 white) and glue, drawing and colouring materials, geographical reference books.

What to do
Show the children the guide books and brochures you have collected and discuss holidays the children have been on. Discuss the idea of a holiday spent touring through a number of countries. Discuss the different types of transport you might use.

Show the children the wall map of Europe and tell them that they are going to plan a package holiday tour which will introduce people to the continent of Europe. Explain that the children's part of the job is to design and write the advertising poster for a holiday which will take people to six European countries – Spain, Italy, France, Germany, the UK and Ireland.

Ask individuals to come to the front and to help you to decide on various options for routes around these six countries. Use the Blu-Tack and string to mark these various routes. Explain to the children that the tourists must visit the six capitals on their holiday and that they must also visit the Mediterranean, the Alps, the Rhine and the North Sea.

Once the children have understood the principle, give them each a copy of photocopiable page 122 and ask them to plan their own route on the map, numbering all the places listed at the bottom in the correct places as they do so.

Give out the poster paper and ask the children to cut out their map and stick it on the poster. The children then design the rest of the poster around the map by drawing pictures of features like the Alps and the Rhine and by writing inviting information about some of the places that those who take the holiday tour will see. Geographical reference books will be needed to support the activity.

Suggestion(s) for extension
Some children will be capable of researching for the posters using information books, atlases, CD-ROM and other information reference systems. Encourage these children to research their tour routes as extensively as possible.

Suggestion(s) for support
You could put children into small research groups. Each one of them could do a poster for one country instead of for all six. You could simply limit the activity to the completion of the map on the photocopiable sheet.

Mapping places

Assessment opportunities

You could present the children with a test style of activity using more copies of photocopiable page 122 as a follow up activity to the poster making. If the children can correctly identify and label the features on the photocopiable sheet, they are satisfying the Key Stage 2 requirements with respect to place knowledge in Europe.

Opportunities for IT

The children could research information for their posters using CD-ROM encyclopaedias, atlases and other information packs as well as the Internet. A scanned or clipart map of Europe could be used within a drawing package, and labelled using the text facilities. Children could use a package like Auto-Route to help them plan their route around Europe with the distances and times taken. Pictures could be scanned from travel brochures or other CD-ROM picture collections. The final poster could be created using a desktop publishing package or a drawing package.

Instead of a poster children could work in groups to write a guidebook for the tour of Europe, including other information such as likely weather statistics, currency and information about the places visited. They could use a desktop publishing package to write and present their information in an interesting and informative way. Some children might be able to make their own electronic presentation using multi-media authoring software.

Display ideas

The children's completed posters could be displayed as though in a travel agent's window. Incorporate the map of Europe in your display and ensure that you have labelled all of the 16 places referred to on the map on photocopiable page 122.

Come and meet Europe

Name _____   Date _____

▲ Put these numbers in the correct boxes on the map.

1. The Alps
2. Berlin
3. Dublin
4. France
5. Germany
6. Ireland
7. Italy
8. London
9. Madrid
10. Mediterranean Sea
11. North Sea
12. Paris
13. River Rhine
14. Rome
15. Spain
16. United Kingdom

Other aspects of the Geography PoS covered

1a, d; 3a, e; 4; 5a.

Reference to photocopiable sheet

Photocopiable page 122 contains a map of Europe based on National Curriculum Map B with 16 boxes to be filled in with numbers. The missing place names are listed at the bottom of the sheet to help the children. The map can be cut from the photocopiable sheet and incorporated in a poster advertising a European tour holiday.

HOLLAND   See Europe!   ITALY   Pisa   FRANCE

WHERE IN THE WORLD?

To have a basic knowledge of the world and to be able to identify certain features on a world map.

†† *Small, even-numbered groups.*

🕐 *10 minutes for discussion; 20 minutes to devise questions; 15 minutes for the quiz activity.*

Previous skills/knowledge needed

Children should be acquainted with maps and should already be well aware of the world map. Children should be able to use the contents and index pages of atlases. Some collaborative work will be necessary.

Key background information

During Key Stage 2 children are expected to acquire a basic knowledge of the world map (National Curriculum Map C). They are expected to be able to identify:

▲ the four oceans (Atlantic, Pacific, Arctic and Indian);

▲ the seven continents (North America, South America, Africa, Europe, Antarctica, Asia and Oceania);

▲ eight of the world's nations (Canada, USA, Brazil, Russian Federation, China, India, Indonesia and Australia);

▲ six major world cities (New York, Buenos Aires, Paris, Cairo, Bombay and Sydney);

▲ the Suez and Panama Canals;

▲ three major mountain ranges (Rockies, Andes and Himalayas);

▲ the Sahara Desert;

▲ three major rivers (Mississippi, Amazon and Nile);

▲ the Equator (0° latitude) and Prime Meridian (0° longitude);

▲ the North and South Poles;

▲ the Tropics of Cancer and Capricorn.

The National Curriculum provides this guidance so that it can be guaranteed that children will have a basic knowledge of the world on which to base their thematic studies.

Preparation

You will need a minimum of two world atlases which contain at least some information about all of the above points of reference. The atlases should be the same to make the activity fair. Each group will need two copies of photocopiable page 123, some paper and writing materials.

Resources needed

At least two (preferably up to eight) atlases, at least two copies of photocopiable page 123 (enlarged if necessary) for each group, paper and writing materials.

What to do

Divide the class into two equal teams of two, three or four children and provide the two teams with the same atlas resources (it doesn't matter how many atlases as long as the teams have the same resources). Provide each team with a photocopy of page 123 which has a world map with all of the points of reference present but missing their labels. The missing labels are available at the bottom of the photocopiable sheet. The two teams start by copying all of the label numbers into the correct places.

Tell the teams to choose 20 of the points of reference listed and design 20 questions where the answer to each question is one of the points of reference on the map. An example might be:

– 'In which country are the cities Nanking, Canton and Shanghai?'

– 'China.'

Tell them that the answers to all the questions must be in the atlases. The contents and index pages of the atlases may well help both to design the questions and find the answers.

Once both the teams in a group have designed their 20 questions the teams can sit opposite each other and take turns to ask their questions. The teams could keep their questions secret from the other teams and take it in turns to 'play' each other in a league. If you are considering doing this, make sure you group your teams in terms of mixed ability, with more able children supporting the less able.

Mapping places

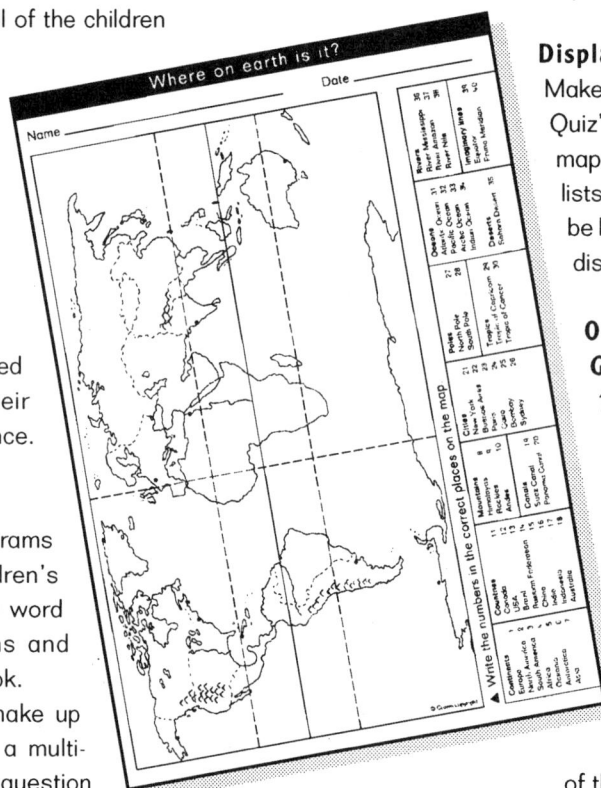

Suggestion(s) for extension

This activity could be used with information sources other than atlases with children using information books, computer information packages and sources like travel guides. More able children could write a geographical quiz book which could even be sent through to another class.

Suggestion(s) for support

Mixed ability groups will enable all of the children to make their own contribution. It may be that you, another adult or an older pupil from another class, need to 'chair' the quiz session to ensure fair play and that all children have a turn to ask and answer questions.

Assessment opportunities

Photocopiable page 123 can be used with individuals to check on their knowledge of the points of reference.

Opportunities for IT

There is a range of computer programs which can be used to test children's world knowledge. Children could word process their lists of questions and answers to make a class quiz book.

Alternatively, children could make up their own interactive quiz using a multi-media authoring package. Each question could be set up with three possible answers. When the child clicks on the right answer they are congratulated, maybe with sound effects or a message and then they can go to the next question. If they get the answer wrong they are shown where that place is and can go back to the question and try again. Each child could add one question to the quiz using the information they have researched so that the completed quiz can be used by the class.

Display ideas

Make a wall display entitled 'Our World Quiz'. Centred around a large world map, this could include each team's lists of questions. The answers could be hidden beneath flaps to make the display a little more inviting.

Other aspects of the Geography PoS covered

1d; 3e.

Reference to photocopiable sheet

Photocopiable page 123 is a world map with the Key Stage 2 points of reference included but not labelled. The labels are included at the bottom of the sheet to assist children as they complete the labelling of the map.

Studying your locality

Children need to learn about their own locality and to develop a responsible attitude towards it. Concentrating on a geographically constrained area around your school offers opportunities to involve children in practical activities which help them to develop a meaningful 'sense of place' and to compare their locality with other localities.

Study of the local area should also be set in a wider geographical context, within its region and country. Links into and out of the locality (buses, sewers, telephone wires and railway lines) should be examined. Children can begin to appreciate the patterns (different types of land and building use) and processes (how the water which falls on the school roof eventually returns to the sea) which exist within a relatively confined area. They must be involved in asking key geographical questions which help them to understand these patterns and processes and they must begin to understand and form opinions on key issues in the locality.

The school's locality presents a context to learn and practise geographical skills and to study themes such as 'rivers', 'weather', 'settlements' and 'environmental change'. Consider the wide variety of fieldwork opportunities presented by the locality and share ideas with colleagues.

A key resource in the study of your locality will be a variety of large scale maps showing your school, residential areas and other features in the area.

YOUR LOCALITY

To appreciate the extent of your school's locality.

†† *Whole class discussion, individuals.*

🕐 *10 minutes for the introductory discussion; 15 minutes to draw maps; 20 minutes for the photocopiable sheet activity.*

Previous skills/knowledge needed

Children will require some knowledge of the area around their school. They will need to be able to draw local features from memory.

Key background information

It is important that children begin to appreciate what is meant by the word 'local'. This is a relative term, of course, but it is worth developing the National Curriculum's Key Stage 2 definition (see Introduction). Children may know the area around their homes fairly intimately, as they might the area around their school. They will know the route to school if they walk it and they may know the area around the homes of close friends and grandparents, the local park and the shops.

Children will have a much more 'watered down' knowledge of the areas beyond these places (such as, the town, the suburb or the immediate area around their village) and a quite abstract, understanding of the rest of their country and the world.

Children need a sound understanding of their own locality so that they can apply what they have learned to help them understand other localities.

Preparation

Obtain or make a large scale map of the area surrounding your school. Make copies of photocopiable page 124 for each child. Identify the important human features (for example, house, road, letter box, bridge, park, hedge, car) and physical features (for example, hill, valley, stream, cliff, river) in the area and prepare a list of these and of some of the less obvious features of the area.

Resources needed

Map of the local area (the larger the scale the better), a reference list of local physical and human geographical features, copies of photocopiable page 124 for each child, paper, drawing, writing and colouring materials.

What to do

Ask the class what they think the word 'local' means. Where have they heard the word? Is it used regularly in any context in your area (local paper/local pub/local church and so on)?

Explain that, as a class, you are going to decide what is local and what is not. See if any of the children can tell you of things in your area which they would say are not local.

Ask each child to think of the area around your school and to have a go at drawing a simple map of the area. Emphasise that the map should show the locality of the *school* and not the locality of their home as this may be different, particularly for children living a distance from the school. Tell the children that they can consult the local map to help them remember where the roads run (you could even photocopy the appropriate section of the map for pairs of children to refer to at their table, but make sure that your school has the appropriate LEA licence to allow you to do this).

The emphasis should be on where the 'edge' of the locality is and on which features the locality contains. Encourage the children to add local features to their maps and to colour their maps in.

When this has been completed, ask the children to colour those places which exist in the school's local area on photocopiable page 124. Explain that the features may look very different to those on the sheet. Then ask the children to draw pictures of the following places from their local area on a separate sheet: the quietest place, the busiest road, the largest building and the smallest building.

Suggestion(s) for extension

Children could extend the photocopiable sheet on to an extra piece of paper following the same format in identifying other features of the locality which they see as important.

Studying your locality

Suggestion(s) for support

Children who have difficulty in comprehending their locality can be supported by using photographic sources. It is well worth making a bank of pictures of features in your locality. You could take the children out on a walk around the locality to further support their understanding.

Assessment opportunities

The children's completed maps will show whether they can demonstrate the geographical extent of the school's locality. Completed copies of photocopiable page 124 will show whether they understand which features are in the locality.

Opportunities for IT

The children could use a mapping package or drawing program to draw their locality maps. If children have taken photographs of features of the locality they could be put on to a KODAK CD-ROM. This means the photographs can be added to the computer drawn maps, or used as a basis for writing using a word processor.

Alternatively, children could create a multi-media presentation using an authoring package which combines a locality map, pictures, text about the features, and a spoken commentary recorded using a microphone attached to the computer.

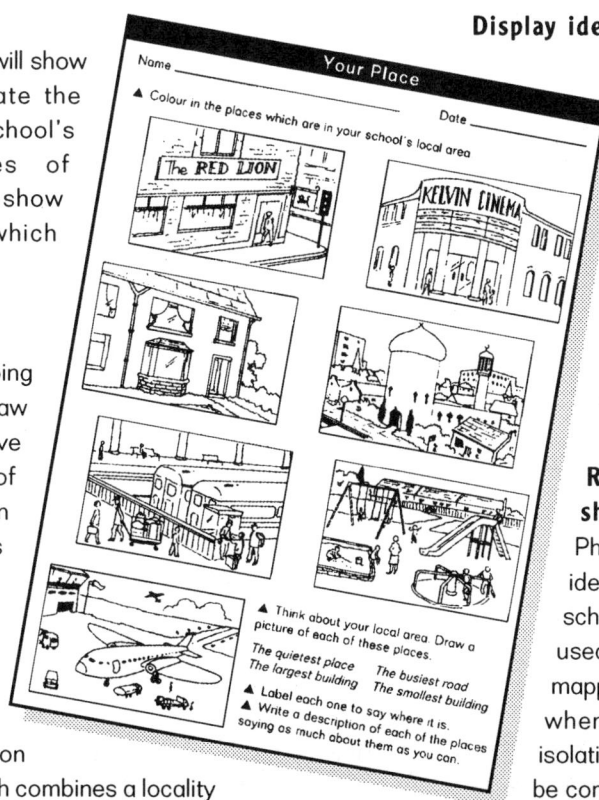

Display ideas

Display each child's finished map and photocopiable sheet together mounted on the same piece of backing paper. Incorporate the large scale map of the locality and any photographs of the locality.

Other aspects of the Geography PoS covered

1d; 3a, c, d; 5a.

Reference to photocopiable sheet

Photocopiable page 124 is used to identify significant buildings in your school's locality. The sheet should be used in conjunction with the children mapping the area and is very effective when used by children working in isolation as the varied results can then be compared to great effect.

51

🌳 PHYSICAL FEATURES

To recognise the physical features of your school's locality.

†† *Group, class, individuals.*

🕐 *10 minutes for discussion; 30 minutes for a walk in local area; 20 minutes for the photocopiable sheet activity.*

Previous skills/knowledge needed

Children should have a reasonable knowledge of the local area around the school and preferably will have visited any local parks and open spaces.

Key background information

Physical geography is concerned with the Earth and its atmosphere: the rocks it is made of; the soils which cover it; the vegetation which grows in those soils; its weather systems; the effects of water and other weathering agents on the Earth's surface; and the landforms which result from these processes.

Children should be aware of any rock or stone features in their locality, of any water features such as streams, rivers or ponds, and of any major areas of soil and vegetation. They need to consider the location of the highest and lowest points in their locality, which bits are flat and where the steepest parts of any slopes are.

Preparation

Collect a range of images of different physical environments (for example, a desert, a mountain range, open moorland). Prepare to take the children on a walk around your locality which includes any place where there is direct evidence of the physical world. Examples might include any streams, open ground, rock outcrops or simply open parkland (including soil, rock, natural water). Prepare copies of photocopiable page 125 for each child to use in follow-up to the walk.

Resources needed

A range of pictures showing different physical environments, adult support for taking the children out of class, copies of photocopiable page 125 for each child, writing and colouring materials.

What to do

Show the children your collection of pictures of different physical environments and discuss what the world can look like when there are no buildings, roads and other human-made features covering it up. Discuss what your local area might look like if you could remove all of the buildings and roads. Tell the children that they are going to be detectives and that they are going to go on a walk to find evidence of what their locality would look like without these things.

Take the children on your pre-planned route and ask them to identify any places where the physical world (soil, rock, natural water) remains evident. As you walk, ask the children to tell you if they notice any slopes. Congratulate any children who 'discover' the types of feature you are looking for.

On return to the classroom give each child a copy of photocopiable page 125 and ask them to draw what the locality really looks like in the upper box and what they imagine it would look like, without all the human features which cover it, in the lower box. Suggest that the views might be as they would appear from a caveman's view from a hilltop or a helicopter hovering above and to one side of the locality as depicted in the illustrations on the sheet.

Studying your locality

Suggestion(s) for extension
You could give children copies of a large scale map of your locality while they are on the walk. Using clipboards and writing materials, they could annotate these maps with notes about the physical environment and then use them to help with the drawing activity back in the classroom.

Suggestion(s) for support
Children who have real difficulty with this activity could be provided with a photograph which shows a building or road in an otherwise unspoilt environment and copy it without the building or road.

Assessment opportunities
Use the finished drawings on the photocopiable sheets to assess how well the children can recognise the physical features which give your locality its character. Asking the children to write descriptions of what they think their locality would look like without buildings can support your assessment.

Opportunities for IT
The children could create a multi-media presentation showing the physical features of their locality using an authoring package. This could combine a scanned map of the locality, pictures scanned from photographs or from a KODAK CD-ROM, a spoken commentary recorded using a microphone attached to the computer and moving images made with a video camera.

If there were no buildings...
Name _____ Date _____
▲ Draw what your locality looks like now...

▲ Draw what your locality would have looked like before people had ever changed it.

When you draw your locality, imagine you are looking down on to it from the side.

Display ideas
The completed sheets could be displayed to show the range of interpretations of how the area would appear without its buildings and roads. Children could produce a larger, artistic version of this to form the focus of the display. Papier mâché models could be made showing the children's interpretations of the locality now and as it would be without the changes made by humankind.

Other aspects of the Geography PoS covered
1b; 2a–c; 3a, b; 4.

Reference to photocopiable sheet
Photocopiable page 125 is used following detailed observation of the physical features of the locality. Children imagine they are looking from above and to the side of their locality. They draw their locality as it appears in reality and how they imagine it would appear if all the buildings, roads and other human features were removed.

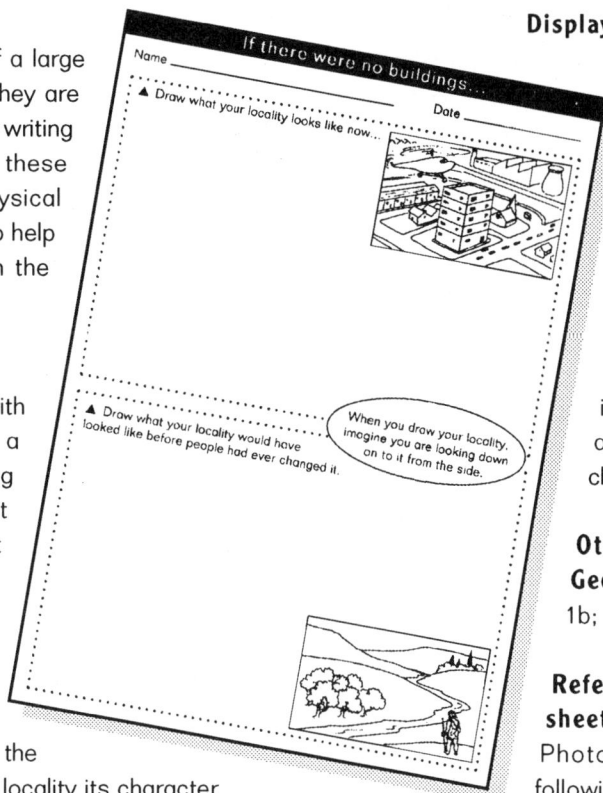

HUMAN FEATURES
To understand the range of human features which provide the children's locality with its character.
†† *Individuals.*
⏱ *15 minutes for the discussion and brainstorm; 30 minutes design activity; 10 minutes for the closing discussion.*

Previous skills/knowledge needed
Children will require some simple knowledge of their own locality and will benefit from any experience that they may have had of drawing buildings.

Key background information
A large part of the character of a locality will result from the human-made parts of the environment. These will include:
▲ residential features such as houses and flats;
▲ retail features such as shops and markets;
▲ places of work such as offices and factories;
▲ leisure places such as swimming pools and parks, and;
▲ transport features such as roads and car parks.
When these features are added together they give a locality its character.

53

GEOGRAPHY KS2: PLACES

Preparation

Collect any guidebooks or pamphlets that you might have about places of different types (for example, local village guides, places you have visited on holiday). Consider arranging a walk around the local area.

Resources needed

Copy of photocopiable page 126 for each child and prepare writing, drawing and colouring materials.

What to do

Talk to the children about what a guidebook is and tell them that they are going to design the front cover of a guidebook for your locality. You could spend some time sharing any guidebooks you have collected with the children.

Discuss the human features of your locality and tell the children that their guidebook will only cover these features. Brainstorm the main residential, retail, work, leisure and transport features of your own locality. Encourage a wide range of ideas and see whether the children can think of features which are in more than one of these categories or in none of them.

Give out the photocopiable sheets with the guidebook cover template printed on it and explain that the children have to make a colourful, neat and attractive front page for their local guidebook. Each child has to think of one residential, one retail and one work building, one leisure place and one transport feature. They draw their school in the oval section and write the name of their locality in the title section. Encourage the children to work as individuals and to draw the places of their personal choice.

Once the children have finished, ask each child to show their completed cover to the rest of the class. Enjoy sharing the different ideas. A follow up to this activity is to involve the children in writing sections of their guidebook for each of the pictures on the cover.

Suggestion(s) for extension

Children capable of extending the activity a little further could consider the route that they would use to take visitors to the locality on a tour around the features they have drawn on their covers. They could make a map of this route to go inside their guide.

Suggestion(s) for support

The best possible support for children who find this activity difficult is to take them on a walk around the locality so that they can actually see and perhaps draw the buildings. Photographs of parts of the local area would also be helpful.

Assessment opportunities

The group discussion will provide you with the best assessment opportunity. Note down which children can demonstrate, through their explanation of their work, an understanding of the way that their locality's features give the area its character.

Opportunities for IT

The children could work in pairs or small groups with a word processor or desktop publishing package to create a class guidebook of the human features in the locality. Each page will need a title picture and text to describe the feature. If a desktop publishing package is used a template or master page can be set up in advance to provide a consistent layout to the pages. Alternatively, children can arrange frames on each page in a way that they think best suits the text and type of picture they have. Other children could design a cover and index for the guidebook.

Display ideas

The completed front covers make an excellent wall display. Include any writing that the children may have done for the inside of the guidebooks or even make the completed books up and display them in the style of a travel agent's on display shelves.

Other aspects of the Geography PoS covered

1b; 3a, f; 9b.

Reference to photocopiable sheet

Photocopiable page 126 provides a template for the front cover of a guidebook to the children's locality. Children draw and colour in major features of their locality and give the front cover a title.

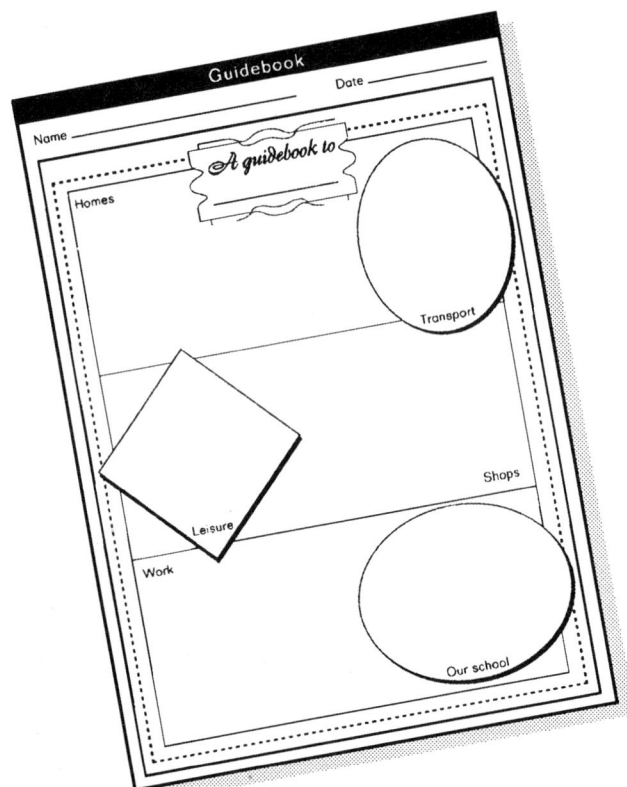

YOUR LOCALITY'S ENVIRONMENT

To recognise the importance of environmental issues in giving your locality its character.

†† *Class, individuals.*

🕐 *15 minutes for the discussion and explanation; 40 minutes for data collection and graphing.*

Previous skills/knowledge needed
Children will need to be capable of completing a simple table of information and turning that information into a graphed result.

Key background information
Children should recognise that their locality's character is as much a result of issues concerning the quality of its environment as the physical and human features which make it up. The environmental quality of a given place is a very subjective and personal thing. There are certain factors which may be commented on or even measured, for example:
▲ levels of air, soil and water pollution;
▲ levels of noise pollution;
▲ aesthetic qualities – is the area 'pleasing to the senses'?
▲ diversity and success of flora and fauna.

An issue real to most primary schools concerns which methods children use to get to school and the methods that they would like to use. It is hoped that children will end up recognising issues like congestion, physical fitness, social interaction among parents and air pollution by cars. Children can relate directly to the problems caused by the private car

as a method of delivering children to school. They see the congestion, and they are aware of the air pollution and noise pollution caused by such cars.

Preparation
Make copies of photocopiable pages 127 and 128 for each child. Collect newspaper articles about environmental issues in your locality.

Resources needed
Newspaper articles about environmental issues in your locality, a copy of photocopiable pages 127 and 128 for each child, drawing materials.

What to do
Talk to the children about the different methods of transport used to travel to school. Explain to them why you use the method you do and discuss why we use different methods. These might include:
▲ using cars because of distance;
▲ walking because we do not have a car;
▲ bus because we are on the bus route;
or more complicated reasons like:
▲ car because crossing local roads is dangerous;
▲ walking because accompanying adult uses the opportunity to walk the dog;
▲ car because neighbouring friend comes by car anyway.

Studying your locality

Using their copies of photocopiable page 127, ask each child to complete the tick chart against the class list showing which method of transport (walk, bicycle, taxi, car or bus) each member of the class normally uses. This data is then transferred to a tally and number chart for each of the transport categories.

Talk to the children about their results and discuss whether any of the children would like to come to school using one of the other methods if they could choose to. Lead the children into discussing the polluting effects of cars and the benefits to health of walking. Talk about any congestion issues on your local roads, particularly referring to any problems at the beginning and end of the school day.

Now ask the children to complete the second part of photocopiable page 127 where they record the method of transport that each child would prefer to use if they could and then the tally and number chart.

Explain to the children that this information would all be far easier to see if it were graphed. Get each child to complete the graphs on photocopiable page 128 using the data they have collected on sheet 127. Discuss how a good graph has a title, a label for each axis, labels along each axis and is clear and accurate.

Suggestion(s) for extension
Challenge children who produce good graphs to interpret their graphs. They should write descriptions of what the two graphs show and try to explain any differences between them.

Suggestion(s) for support
Children could carry out this activity in pairs with one more able child supporting one less able child.

Assessment opportunities
The two photocopiable sheets provide evidence of the children's ability to collect and graph data but it is particularly important that the children are given a chance to demonstrate what any differences between the two graphs mean. Ask the children to write brief explanations. Look at the children's completed photocopiable sheet graphs to see how accurately they have completed them.

Opportunities for IT
Children could use simple graphing software to collect and display the information about actual and preferred means of transport.

Alternatively, the class could create a database showing the information which could include other factors. The fieldnames could include:

Name	David
Sex	Boy
Distance to school	2.5 miles
Actual transport	Car
Preferred	Bike
Reason do not travel this way	Too dangerous

Some databases such as Junior Pinpoint have a tokenised field so that children are presented with a selection of possible answers. This cuts down ambiguity and entry mistakes which makes for a more consistent and usable database.

The children can then interrogate the data to answer the following questions and the results can be plotted on different types of graphs for comparison and interpretation:

▲ Who travels the furthest to school?

▲ How many children travel by car?

▲ Is there a connection between the distance and transport used?

▲ Do boys walk more than girls?

Display ideas
Make large versions of some of the finished graphs. This can be done in 3D using large Unifix, Multilink, Centilink, LEGO or DUPLO blocks for each unit of the graph. Children could use junk card boxes of the same size (for example, shoe boxes) and they could draw on the unit that each box represents (a car, a bus, someone walking and so on).

Other aspects of the Geography PoS covered
1b; 2a–c; 4.

Reference to photocopiable sheets
Photocopiable page 127, 'Getting to school', is used for children to collect information on the methods, and preferred methods, that their class travel to school. They fill in a tick table and complete a tally and number chart. Photocopiable page 128, 'Travel bar graphs', is used to graph the two sets of information generated using sheet 127.

HUMAN ACTIVITY IN YOUR LOCALITY

To recognise that human activities in your locality relate to its features.

†† *Individuals, group.*

🕐 *20 minutes for the discussion; 30 minutes for the mapping activity.*

Previous skills/knowledge needed

Children will benefit from any previous work on transport systems and work using the local map.

Key background information

Children should be able to recognise major human and physical geographical features and environmental issues in their locality. It is important that children begin to recognise that these affect where other features are located. Bus routes tend to link major residential areas with services and places of work. They are a response to a need brought about by human and physical features. Bus routes became particularly important when a lot of.urban residential areas moved out from the middle of town centres and then when places of work ceased to be close to existing residential areas. Key Stage 2 children are very capable of understanding the plight of those who do not own private cars, particularly the elderly, and can be encouraged to empathise with them and to see the need for an effective public transport system.

Preparation

Make copies of photocopiable page 129 for each child. Obtain a large scale map of your school's locality and, if possible, a local bus timetable.

Resources needed

A copy of photocopiable sheet 129 for each child, a large scale local map, copies of local bus timetables, paper.

What to do

Establish a list of key places within the locality or within easy reach of the locality. These might include:

▲ Regularly used shops – food shops, newsagents, post offices, supermarkets;

▲ Occasionally used shops – clothing shops, furniture shops, hairdressers;

▲ Employers – major places of work;

▲ Education – schools, nurseries and playgroups;

▲ Medical – doctors, dentists, clinics and hospitals;

▲ 'Busy leisure' – parks, playgrounds, sports centres, swimming baths, gyms and youth clubs;

▲ 'Quiet' leisure – cinemas, restaurants, cafes and pubs;

▲ Worship – churches and mosques.

The children list the residential areas and the different places to visit in the relevant places on the lower part of photocopiable page 129. Discuss how people travel to and from these places and how all of these places are linked. Encourage a wide range of suggestions.

Show the children the large scale local map and talk about how the roads link places together. See if any of the children can tell you where the bus stops and routes are.

Each child now either copies or draws from memory a map of the local area around the school using the box at the top of photocopiable page 129. They only need to draw the roads and the major features that were brainstormed in the earlier session as well as the main places on the map where people live.

Next, tell the children to draw where *they* would locate bus stops and where *they* would run the bus routes. They can mark the routes as lines on the map and fill in the key with symbols accordingly. Explain that the bus company would only be able to run two bus routes and locate four bus stops in this area and that they will, therefore, have to think carefully about planning the routes so that most people will be able to use the bus. Children can write a short explanation of their planned routes on a separate sheet of paper.

Suggestion(s) for extension

Challenge the children by asking them to use the scale on the map to calculate the distance of each of the features they have marked on the map, from its nearest bus stop.

Suggestion(s) for support

Some children will find the map drawing challenging. You could make multiple photocopies of the local map (provided that you have the appropriate photocopy licence) and allow the children to stick trimmed sections on to their sheet once they have drawn on their routes and bus stops.

Assessment opportunities

Their response to the section at the foot of each child's photocopiable sheet shows how well they recognise that geographical features affect decisions about the location of other human activities.

Opportunities for IT

The children could use a graphing package or database to record and display the times taken to reach different places in their locality. The data could be collected in several ways:

▲ time taken from home to the place
▲ time taken to reach nearest bus stop
▲ time taken to travel by car
▲ time taken for total journey time by bus (walking and on bus)
▲ time taken by bicycle

The results could be discussed and the environmental implications for the different ways of transport examined in detail.

Buildings people in our area use

Name _____

A map of the local area around our school _____ Date _____

Key
- Roads
- Bus route
- ⑤ Bus stop

Homes

Employers

Busy leisure

Shops that are used often

Education

Quiet leisure

Shops that are not used often

Medical

Worship

▲ Write on explanation of the bus route you have chosen on a separate sheet of paper.

Display ideas

Create a large tabletop display based on a 3D model of your area and its streets. The children can make model bus stops, key buildings (like the school) and buses and they could even mark a dotted line to show their favourite projected bus route.

Other aspects of the Geography PoS covered

3c, d; 5a; 9b, c.

Reference to photocopiable sheet

Photocopiable page 129 is used by children to record brainstormed information on local residential areas and the places people visit. Children map this information in the map box, complete the key and then use the map to plan two bus routes and four bus stop locations. The children then justify the routes they have designed on a separate sheet of paper.

⬛ CHANGE IN YOUR LOCALITY

To recognise and to be able to explain what is changing in your own locality.
†† *Small groups within class.*
🕐 *5 minutes for the introduction; 20 minutes for the activity on the photocopiable; 30 minutes to create the newspaper article.*

Previous skills/knowledge needed

Children should be acquainted with newspapers and with the idea of writing in a journalistic way. They need experience of writing non-fiction involving drafting, editing and rewriting.

Key background information

It is important that children recognise the processes involved in geography and that things change through time. Geography is not simply about a 'snap-shot' of what is happening in a place at one moment in time, it is concerned with the changing processes and patterns existing in different places. Changing processes might include an increasing volume of road traffic or a stream being re-routed into a straightened culvert. Changing patterns might include changes in land and building use such as farmland changing to residential use or industrial land becoming derelict or changing to retail use. Children should be led into enquiring about the world which they otherwise might take to be rather static and un-changing.

Preparation

Consider your school's local area and identify some human, physical or environmental changes which *have* happened, *are* happening or are *likely to* happen. Issues might include:

▲ land being 'swallowed up' for new housing;

▲ increasingly heavy traffic on a local road;

▲ gardens in the area being less well tended;

▲ a by-passing scheme;

▲ a local shop closing.

Make a note of these, they may be important once you start working with the children. Prepare a large scale map of your locality and find paper suitable for the children to write newspaper articles on.

Resources needed

Large scale map of your locality, large pieces of white paper, a stock of smaller pieces of paper, glue, scissors and writing materials, a copy of photocopiable page 130 for each child.

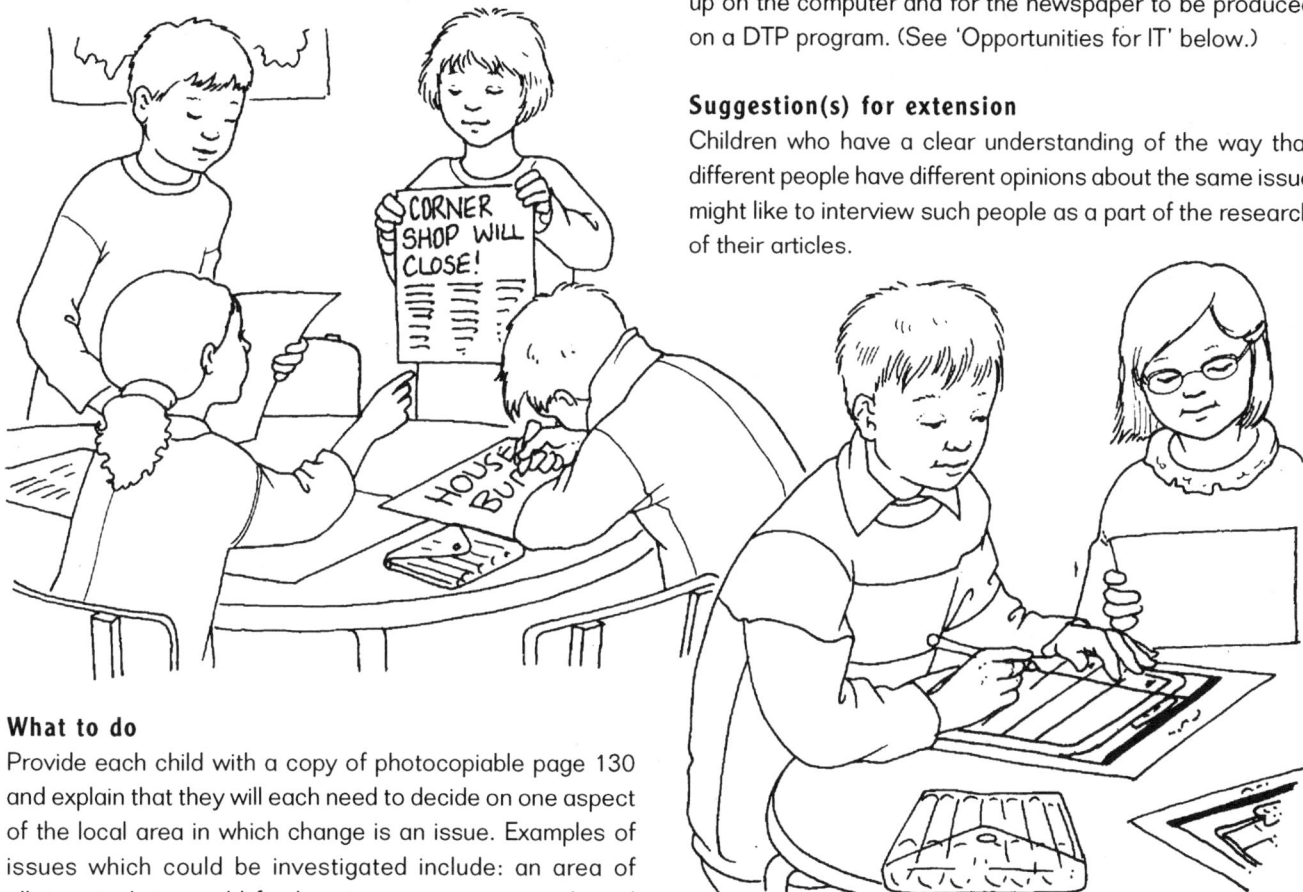

What to do

Provide each child with a copy of photocopiable page 130 and explain that they will each need to decide on one aspect of the local area in which change is an issue. Examples of issues which could be investigated include: an area of allotments being sold for housing, a new improved road junction taking a small amount of land from a green area, a bus route changing, closure of a local shop. The children write their chosen issue at the top of the sheet and then complete each of the following sections:

▲ WHAT – What is the change?

▲ WHEN – When is the change in the past/present/future?

▲ WHERE – Where in the locality is this change?

▲ WHO – Who can tell me more about the change?

　　　　 – Who will have opinions about the change?

▲ HOW – How is the change going to take place?

▲ WHY – What are the reasons for this change?

These questions ensure that the children have considered the issue properly and prepare them to write a newspaper article on the subject.

You are aiming at producing a whole-class newspaper with as many different articles as possible. The title of the newspaper could be 'Your area... past, present and future.'

Each issue is written up in newspaper style format using the photocopiable page as a resource. Each article will need a headline, text, a picture and would be best written on to A4 white paper. The finished articles can be cut out and stuck on to a larger piece of paper (or several pieces) to make the finished newspaper. Gluing all of the articles on to A3 paper and then photocopying it produces a pleasing final result.

An alternative to the handwriting and cut and stick version of this activity is to get each writing team to type their articles up on the computer and for the newspaper to be produced on a DTP program. (See 'Opportunities for IT' below.)

Suggestion(s) for extension

Children who have a clear understanding of the way that different people have different opinions about the same issue might like to interview such people as a part of the research of their articles.

Suggestion(s) for support

Children may benefit from working in small 'writing teams' of two or more children. In this way the burden of writing an article which covers all of the areas identified in photocopiable page 130 can be shared out.

Assessment opportunities

Children could write a short review of each other's pieces of work. Each child could read out their original article and then their reviewer could read the review. Listen carefully and make notes about whether each child recognises that change is an issue in your locality. Keep copies of photocopiable page 130 as added evidence.

Change checklist

Name _____
The Issue: _____
Date _____

WHAT? ?	What is the change?
WHEN?	Is the change in the past/present/future?
WHERE?	Where in the locality is this change?
WHO?	Who can tell me more about the change? Who will have opinions about the change?
HOW?	How is the change going to take place?
WHY? ?	What are the reasons for this change?

▲ Use the answers to these questions to help you write your newspaper article.

LINKS WITH WHERE YOU LIVE

To understand the complex links an area has with other places.

†† *Individuals.*

🕐 *10 minutes for the discussion; 25 minutes for the map tracing activity; 15 minutes for the activity on the photocopiable sheet.*

Previous skills/knowledge needed
Children will need to be able to trace from a map using tracing paper.

Key background information
It is particularly important that children are aware of the way that their locality is connected to other places within their area, their region and their country. Places are connected in a myriad of different ways:

▲ telephone cable/radio waves/satellite signals/television signals/cable TV/electronic mail/letter post;

▲ pathways/roads and motorways/railways;

▲ canals/rivers/seaways/tunnels/bridges;

▲ air routes.

Study of these channels of communication will lead to an understanding of some of the patterns and processes operating in geography. Understanding communication routes can help us understand patterns of land use and how and why people take the journeys to work and school that they do.

Preparation
Make A4 photocopies of your school's local 1:25 000 (local) and 1:250 000 (regional) Ordnance Survey maps and a suitable national map such as that found in the front of most

Opportunities for IT
This activity is particularly relevant to the use of the computer and a DTP program. If you are intending the children to use the computer, prepare it, the relevant application and the printer accordingly.

The children could work in groups using a desktop publishing package to write and edit their newspaper page. A template or master page could be set up in advance by the teacher to give a consistent layout.

Children could add pictures, scanned from their own photographs or line drawings, or added from local collections transferred to a KODAK CD-ROM. The work of the groups could be combined to make a class newspaper, using both sides of the newspaper pages.

Display ideas
The finished newspaper should be displayed to the full and, most importantly, read by others. A high street style news stand is a good way of doing this as part of a free-standing display.

Other aspects of the Geography PoS covered
1b; 2b, c; 3a, f; 4.

Reference to photocopiable sheet
Photocopiable page 130 is used to assist children to organise the information for their newspaper articles. Children choose an issue involving change in their local area and answer the questions in the different sections.

road atlases. (Make sure that you have the necessary LEA photocopying licence to do this.) With the first two of these photocopies ensure that your locality is fairly central to the final copies. Collect tracing paper and a variety of coloured felt-tipped pens.

Resources needed

Copies of the three map extracts and tracing paper for each child, pencils, a variety of fairly fine felt-tipped pens, paper, copies of photocopiable page 131 for each child.

What to do

Provide each of the children with a copy of each of the maps and three pieces of tracing paper. Ask the children to draw on where their own home area is. On the 1:25 000 map this might be a small area of shading. On the other two maps it is far more likely to be a simple dot.

Talk to the children about the means of communication shown by each of the maps and then ask them to trace these routeways in pencil. Next ask them to decide on a felt-tipped pen colour for each of the routeway types and to go over the pencil lines carefully using the appropriate colours.

The three finished traced maps can now be labelled with labels for other major settlements and a key for the routeway types. Using tracing paper limits children to recording only the transport routes and settlements. (Routeways might include footpath, bridleway, road, motorway, railway, tramway, canal and navigable river and air routes if there is an airport and you have information on which direction the main flight paths take.) An effective way to organise the completed work is to get the children to stick their three maps and the key on to a large piece of white paper.

Talk to the children about the patterns which their transport route maps show. If you are lucky you may have children who have identified a 'spider's web' type of pattern around your town or area and other settlements.

As follow up to this activity ask the children to complete photocopiable page 131 which involves them in interrogating their maps to answer questions about the routeways and places which connect with your own local area.

Suggestion(s) for extension

Some children will be capable of tracing more subtle lines of communication than others. These might include power transmission lines, cycle ways or actual trunk routes on the national or regional maps.

Suggestion(s) for support

Children who have trouble with the fact that you have photocopied in black and white might be given the original coloured map to work from. The smaller scale maps are generally easier to trace from so you could group children into threes and ask the less able child to work on these maps while the other two do the larger scale maps.

Assessment opportunities

Photocopiable page 131 can be used to assess children's understanding of the broader context in which your locality is placed.

Opportunities for IT

Children could draw the simple routeway-only maps that they have created on to the computer using a drawing program.

Display ideas

Make a large version of each of the maps. Children can use different colours of ribbon or strips of sugar paper to represent different types of routeway and can stick these to the maps.

Other aspects of the Geography PoS covered

1a, c, d; 3d; 4; 5a.

Reference to photocopiable sheet

Photocopiable page 131 asks the children to identify some of the routeways and places identified in their map tracing work. Children have to research information concerned with railways, roads, motorways, transport nodes and settlements which are linked to their own locality. It is hoped that the number of features ticked will increase from the 'local' map to the 'national' map.

THE SAME BUT DIFFERENT

To understand that there are similarities and differences between your locality and other localities.

†† *Pairs.*

🕐 *5 minutes for the introduction; 25 minutes for the poster design; 5 minutes for the class discussion.*

Previous skills/knowledge needed

Children should have studied a locality which contrasts with their own.

Key background information

As children learn geographical skills and themes it is important that they do so in the context of a range of contrasting places. As they do this they will, increasingly, recognise the similarities and differences which exist when places are compared. The place that children know best is their own locality. Children must be able to contrast this with the contrasting UK and contrasting overseas localities studied during the Key Stage. These should be of similar size to your own locality and one should be in the UK and the other in Africa, Asia (excluding Japan), South America or central America (including the Caribbean).

Preparation

Acquaint yourself with the types of place on photocopiable page 132 and collect together any resources you may have on one of the contrasting localities the children have studied in the past.

Resources needed

Copies of photocopiable page 132 for each child, any resources which will support research about the locality being contrasted. Writing and drawing materials.

What to do

Discuss the idea of two places having some characteristics which are similar and others which are different. Stimulate a discussion about what makes your locality 'feel' like your locality.

Explain to the children that they are going to design a poster advertising their own school's locality and a poster advertising the contrasting locality that your class is studying. Show the children the resources you have collected and talk about what makes a good, informative poster. Give each pair two copies of photocopiable page 132 and explain that they have to design pictures in each of the boxes according to the titles.

The titles are:

▲ The place where many people work;
▲ One of the best views;
▲ Where the children go to school;
▲ A typical home;
▲ A good place to enjoy yourself.

Encourage the pairs of children to work as a team, with each child contributing to both posters.

Once each pair has completed their two posters they show them to the rest of the class and describe which things are the same and which are different.

Suggestion(s) for extension

Children can identify other characteristics of the localities which are not already the focus of the posters.

Suggestion(s) for support

Some children will find the activity easier to tackle if you provide them with more picture resources of the localities. Pair your children carefully so that less able children are supported by more able.

Assessment opportunities

Ask children to write a short passage about each of the five pairs of pictures in the two posters (that is, their school's locality and the contrasting locality). Tell them that their writing must focus on what is similar in the two posters and what is different.

GEOGRAPHY
KS2: PLACES

Name _____
Date _____

A great place

The delights of

The place where many people work

Where the children go to school

One of the best views

A typical home

A good place to enjoy yourself

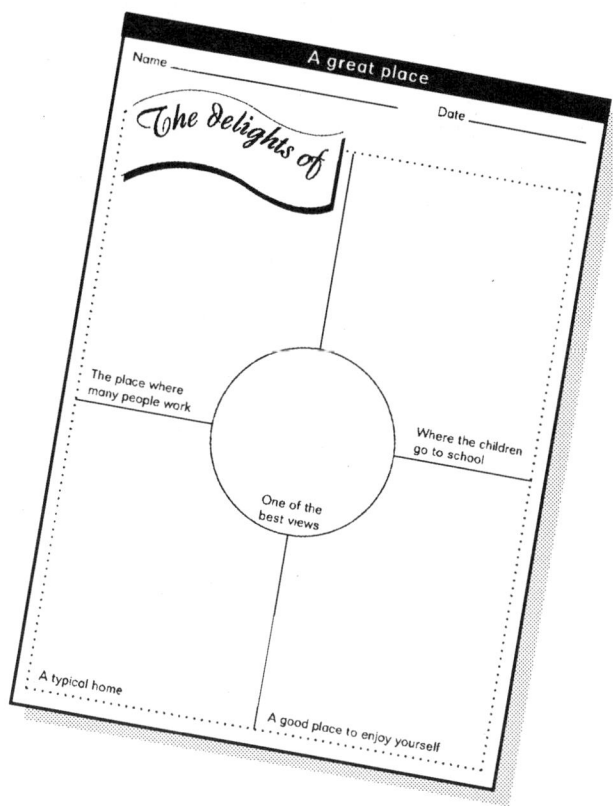

Opportunities for IT

The children could use a drawing package or desktop publishing program to design their poster. They could use an art package to draw their own pictures or scan their own line drawings or photographs of the locality. Alternatively, pictures of contrasting localities could be taken from commercial CD-ROM collections and pictures of the school's locality from a KODAK CD-ROM prepared by the school.

The children can experiment with different layouts for the pictures, changing their size or position and adding text in a variety of fonts and sizes. With a drawing package it is often possible to alter the shape of text to make the poster more interesting.

Display ideas

Display the completed poster designs in a line on card protruding from the wall in a concertina fashion. If you alternate the posters one locality then the other, a viewer looking from one angle will see all the posters for your own locality and a viewer looking from another angle will see all the posters for the contrasting locality.

Other aspects of the Geography PoS covered

3e, 4; 5a.

Reference to photocopiable sheet

Copies of photocopiable page 132 are used by children to create two posters, one advertising their own locality and one advertising a contrasting locality. Titles below the boxes tell the children what each box should show.

THEMES IN YOUR AREA

To recognise characteristics of the local area concerned with rivers, weather, settlement and environmental change.

†† *Four groups.*

🕐 *10–15 minutes for the discussion; 45–60 minutes group collage work.*

Previous skills/knowledge needed

The children will need to have had experience of using large scale maps.

Key background information

The four themes of rivers, weather, settlement and environmental change should be investigated by children during Key Stage 2. These can be studied as separate themes or as a part of work on different localities. Rivers as a theme involves the study of any part of the water cycle including streams, rivers, river features, piping, drains and water treatment facilities. Weather relates to local weather conditions, seasonal variations, and the small scale changes in your locality. Settlement refers to all of the different ways in which people live together, in solitary houses, in hamlets, villages, towns, suburbs, cities and large conurbations. Environmental change refers to how people are preserving, changing and managing aspects of their environment.

Preparation

Ensure that you have the appropriate photocopying licence, then make copies of a large scale map of your locality so that each group of three or four children will have their own. Gather a wide range of collage materials: different coloured and textured fabrics, card, string, yarn and shiny items will all prove useful. Prepare an area of the classroom for cutting and gluing activities. Clear an area of display board and section it into four quarters.

Resources needed

A copy of the large scale map of your area for each group, a wide range of collage materials, scissors, glue, paper, a copy of photocopiable sheet 133 for each child.

What to do

As a class activity, discuss the themes of rivers, weather, settlement and environmental change in the context of your own locality. Brainstorm ideas and information which have any connection with these themes and write resultant words or phrases up on the board.

Explain to the children that they are going to make a large wall collage all about their own locality and that the collage will have four sections to it.

The children will have more difficulty thinking of ideas for some of the themes than for others. The theme of 'Rivers',

63

Studying your locality

for example, is difficult in some localities. If this theme does pose a problem get them to think about where raindrops in their locality end up. The children are within a catchment and there are water channels even if they are human-made and underground.

Each group of children decides which of the four themes they wish to represent in collage form. The children use their copies of photocopiable page 133 to help them design their part of the collage. They use copies of the large scale map of the area to help them think of ideas. The collage is best created in small areas of picture which are then added to the wall display in montage form to make the finished piece of work.

Suggestion(s) for extension

If one theme is more difficult than others in your area, group the children so that more able ones address this theme.

Suggestion(s) for support

Easier themes could be tackled by less able children. You could sub-divide themes up to make them easier to tackle. A less able group might find it easier to tackle 'windy parts of our locality' than 'weather in our locality'. Alternatively, deal with only one theme at a time, thereby producing a much larger, single subject montage.

Assessment opportunities

Children's completed photocopiable sheets, which involve them in identifying key characteristics of their locality with respect to one of the four themes, will provide evidence of their identification of aspects which are a particular feature of, or even unique to, your locality.

Opportunities for IT

Some children could use an art package to create their own pictures of one of the themes in the area. The work of four children could be mounted to form pictures in the same way as the collages.

Display ideas

The activity creates a display in itself. Consider incorporating photographs of the area, written work, the completed photocopiable sheets and the local large scale map into the display.

Other aspects of the Geography PoS covered

3d; 4; 5a–e; 7–10.

Reference to photocopiable sheet

Photocopiable page 133 is used to help children to plan their collage display. The children identify characteristics of their own area according to the themes of rivers, weather, settlements and environmental change by answering key questions on the sheet.

64

GEOGRAPHY KS2: PLACES

Studying a contrasting UK locality

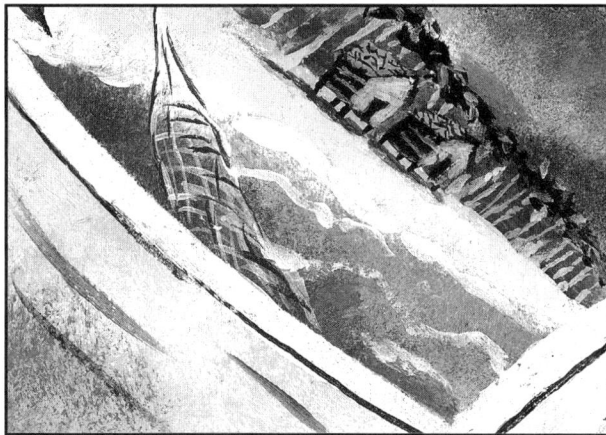

Children should develop their understanding of places by studying at least two similar-sized localities which contrast with their own local area. One of these localities must be in the UK and your aim should be for the children to have an understanding of what it would be like to live there.

Teachers must choose a locality where they can obtain detailed local information. Large scale, detailed maps of this geographical area are one important resource. You could either choose a locality which is close enough for at least one fieldwork visit which involves the children in practical first-hand experiences of the locality (ensure that any nearby locality genuinely contrasts with your own in some respects); or choose a residential fieldwork visit – children can be involved in the practicalities of living in the locality and truly begin to get an idea of what it might be like to live in that place permanently.

Children should be taught about physical and human features in the locality they are studying, but it is also very important that they learn about real issues in that locality and how it is changing.

The thematic studies of rivers, weather, settlement and environmental change should be taught through real places and a contrasting UK locality offers a good opportunity for this. It may be that your choice of contrasting locality partly reflects your desire to teach about one or more of the themes through this place.

references to the activity 'Putting it on the map' and photocopy this amended sheet to give to the children.

Resources needed
Selection of road atlases, reference books and copies of photocopiable page 134 and the amended page 141 for each pair of children. Drawing and writing materials.

What to do
Provide each pair with a selection of reference materials and allow a period of time to examine them. This done, discuss what they can find out from the materials and how best to 'navigate' their way around them by use of the index, contents page, 'go to' page referencing at the side of an atlas map page and introductory location maps.

Tell the children to discuss parts of the UK that they have been to, where they may have relatives or friends or that they know about from books or television. Give the children the photocopiable sheets and ask them to choose two cities, two towns and two villages and to locate them all on the map of the UK. (They should mark the places with the correct symbol and the relevant letter between A and F.) It is a good idea to encourage the children to include any contrasting localities that they have studied or are going to study.

Having marked the six places on the map (page 141) the children can fill in the rest of page 134 listing information gleaned from the reference books and atlases. The final piece of information for each place – 'main ways of earning a living...' – can be extracted from written information in reference books or using picture clues showing, for example, farming, sea fishing, working in industry.

VARIETY IN THE UK

To show that there is an enormous variety of places in the UK.

†† *Pairs.*

🕐 *10 minutes introduction; 30–40 minutes activity.*

Previous skills/knowledge needed
Children must be capable of using reference books (see information below).

Key background information
To help children put their home locality and other UK localities studied in context it is worth involving children in activities which provide a widening range of scales and a wide geographical context (from the immediate area at a large scale to the global at a small scale). The skill of interrogating reference books is a useful one and can support understanding about specific places as well as about variations in settlement size, character and location. Introduce children to as wide a range of reference books on places as you can. These might include topic and guide books on places, encyclopaedias, souvenir brochures as well as 'coffee table' style books such as *The AA Book of the Road*.

Preparation
Gather a selection of road atlases and reference books about the UK or parts of the UK. If possible, make sure that there is material with information about localities that the children have studied in the past or that they are likely to study in the future. Make copies of photocopiable page 134. Use the map of the UK on page 141 for this activity. Delete all

66

Suggestion(s) for extension

You could set criteria for the places the children are to select. One way of doing this would be to stipulate that there should be at least one place from each of the constituent countries of the UK.

Suggestion(s) for support

Pair children so that a less able child is sitting with a child of greater ability. This might be particularly important with respect to reading.

Assessment opportunities

Once children have completed their sheets, ask each pair to tell the rest of their group or class about the places they have chosen. Assess the ability of each child with respect to the investigation of places across a widening range of scales and awareness of how places fit into a wider geographical context. Look particularly for children who have used more than one reference book, who have used the index, contents page and other 'navigation aids' in the materials, and who have gleened information from a wide range of sources within the books, such as photographs, text, maps and diagrams.

Opportunities for IT

Computer CD-ROM packages such as encyclopaedia and atlases can be used to support this activity.

Display ideas

Display the children's completed sheets around a large map of the UK. Ask each child to choose one place that they found particularly interesting from their sheet and link this from the sheet to its location on the large map using thread and map pins.

Other aspects of the Geography PoS covered

1a, d; 3a, d, e; 5e; 9a.

Reference to photocopiable sheets

Photocopiable pages 134 and 141 are used as a central part of this activity. Children locate the six places they have chosen on the UK map on page 141 and fill in the details for those places in the six sections on page 134.

UK LOCALITY – PHYSICAL FEATURES

To recognise the physical features of a contrasting locality in the UK.

†† *Groups.*

🕒 *15 minutes photocopiable sheet as either introductory or follow-up activity; 10 minutes introductory discussion; 25 minutes activity; (field sketching activity in locality optional); 5–10 minutes concluding discussion.*

Previous skills/knowledge needed

Children will need to be able to interpret maps, photographs and other secondary sources relating to the contrasting locality being studied.

Key background information

An important component of understanding a contrasting locality is that children are taught about its physical features – one way of doing this is to visit the locality and to make field sketches – if this is not possible the children can learn much from performing a similar exercise using secondary source material.

Children should be able to identify key features such as:
▲ Relief – hills, valleys, slopes, escarpments, different gradients.

▲ Water features – sea, lakes, ponds, rivers, streams, marshes.

▲ Rock/soil – type of, colour of.

▲ Landforms – cliffs, scree, stream/river channels, meanders, beaches.

If using a field visit, you may need to point out the map symbols relating to certain physical features so that the children can learn how features on the ground relate to those on a map.

Preparation

Collect a variety of photographic images of the locality being studied. The images should include some detail, even if quite subtle, of the physical nature of the area. Provide copies of a large scale map of the area.

Resources needed

A range of images (see 'Preparation'), copies of a large scale map of the locality and photocopiable page 135 for each child, paper, drawing pencils.

What to do

Photocopiable page 135 can be used as an optional introduction to this activity. This type of drawing probably makes it easier for children to identify 'features' than a photograph does. It also gives them practice in 'looking' and may help prepare them for the rest of the activity. Provide each child with one picture of the locality being studied. Each child must keep their picture secret from the rest of the group at this stage. Talk with the children about what their pictures might tell them about the physical features of the area. Such information may be quite subtle and require some careful interpretation to see past the human features which may be obscuring the physical.

Tell the children to re-draw the view in the picture but that their sketch must clearly identify all the physical features that are evident as well as any human ones. This done, tell the children to label all of the physical features very clearly. While the children re-draw the pictures they must remember not to let other members of the group see.

Once all of the children have finished their individual sketches, gather all of the original pictures back in and display them so that everyone can see them. One at a time, the children now show their sketches and the rest of the group try to identify the picture that each one was based on.

Give out the copies of the large scale maps and, holding up the pictures one at a time, encourage the children to identify the location of each view and the direction the person who took the photograph would have been pointing. Get them to mark this information on to their maps (see illustration).

Suggestion(s) for extension

Some children may wish to add a written description of the physical features evident in their sketch as well as the labels. Encourage children to go into as much detail as possible in their sketching.

Suggestion(s) for support

Start the less able children off with the photocopiable sheet to focus them on what 'physical features' are. Before you distribute the pictures arrange them in terms of difficulty and provide these children with more straightforward images.

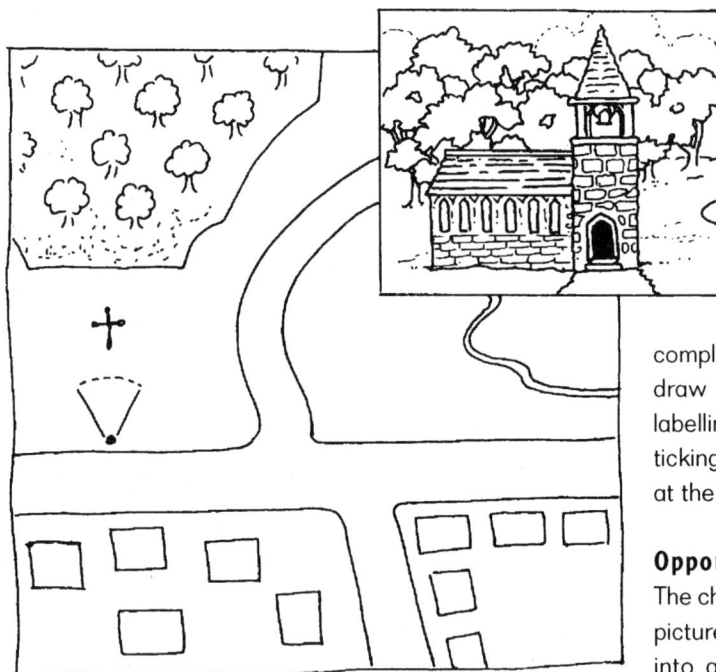

Assessment opportunities

The photocopiable sheet can be used to provide evidence of children's ability to recognise physical features from a complicated image. The children re-draw the picture in sketch form, labelling the physical features and ticking the relevant ones off the list at the side of the sheet.

Opportunities for IT

The children could scan their drawn pictures so that they can be loaded into a drawing package and the physical features labelled. If it is possible to obtain pictures of the locality these can either be scanned or you could get them put on to a KODAK CD-ROM so that they are available in electronic format. It may be possible to download pictures from the Internet.

Display ideas

Have a group vote on the best sketch interpretation and involve the whole group in re-drawing the sketch on a large scale to provide a wall display. An effective interactive display can be made by displaying the original pictures on one side of a display board and the children's sketches on the other. Viewers have to decide which picture goes with which sketch. The answers could be provided under a flap of card.

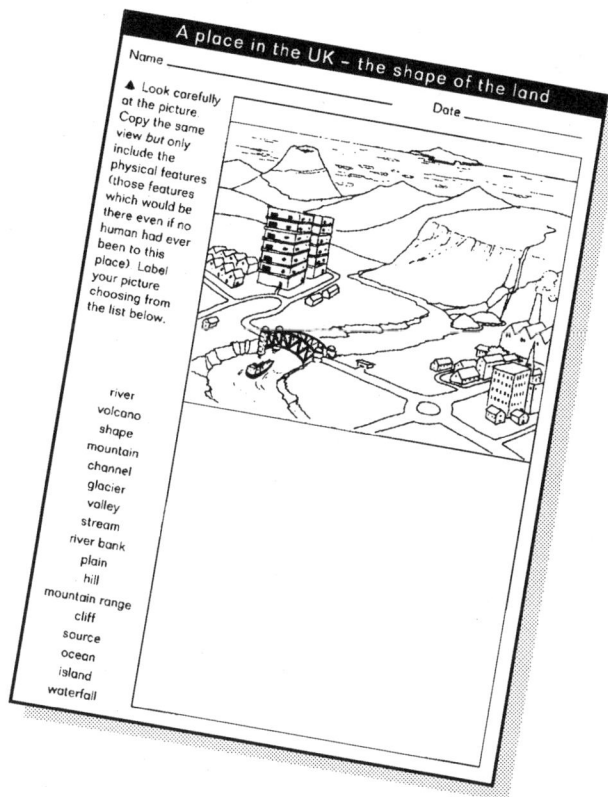

A place in the UK – the shape of the land

Name ___

▲ Look carefully at the picture. Copy the same view but only include the physical features (those features which would be there even if no human had ever been to this place). Label your picture choosing from the list below.

Date ___

river
volcano
shape
mountain
channel
glacier
valley
stream
river bank
plain
hill
mountain range
cliff
source
ocean
island
waterfall

Other aspects of the Geography PoS covered
1b; 2a, c; 3a, d, e.

Reference to photocopiable sheet
Photocopiable page 135 can be used to introduce the activity, as a support, or to assess children's understanding of the physical features evident in the locality being studied. They re-draw the image and label the physical features ticking them off the list at the side of the sheet as they use them.

UK LOCALITY – HUMAN FEATURES

To recognise human features in a contrasting UK locality.
†† *Pairs.*
🕐 *10 minutes introduction; 20 minutes game; 20 minutes 'diary' writing.*

Previous skills/knowledge needed
Children should have studied the human features of their own locality and have an understanding of what a diary is.

Key background information
A key aim for children studying a contrasting locality should be that they develop some idea of what it would be like to live in that place. A locality's human features, those features which are primarily the result of the actions of human beings,

can be considered most effectively when the 'working day' (including voluntary, looking after the sick, mothering and so on) of people resident in the locality is examined. A residential fieldwork visit would provide an excellent opportunity for studying other people's 'working days'. However, children can gain their knowledge from secondary sources.

Human features might include:
▲ Residential features – houses, flats, gardens
▲ Offices – banks, building societies, agencies, town halls, job centres, post offices
▲ Industrial features – factories, industrial parks, mills
▲ Shopping features – shops, shopping centres
▲ Leisure features – parks, sports/leisure centres, golf courses, pitches, playgrounds, swimming baths
▲ Transport features – paths, roads, railways / stations, car parks, bus stations, taxi ranks
▲ Educational features – nurseries, schools, colleges, universities
▲ Medical features – doctors, dentists, clinics, hospitals
▲ Support features – ambulance/fire/police stations.

They would also include the street furniture (post boxes, street lights and so on), vehicles and other everyday items which are a part of people's lives.

Preparation
Make a list of jobs which people do in the contrasting UK locality that the children are studying. Make sure that this includes as wide a range of jobs as possible including those which might be specific to that locality like coal miner, trawlerman and forester, those which might be found in any locality like teacher, shop assistant and nurse as well as activities like voluntary work, raising families and caring. Write the title of each job on a piece of card.

Resources needed
Occupation cards (as referred to above), copies of the diary sheet for each child (photocopiable page 136).

What to do
Discuss the jobs which are done in the contrasting locality. As far as possible, involve the children in connecting jobs referred to with the places where the jobs are carried out. Try to get the children to think of as wide a range of jobs as possible and encourage children who think of slightly unusual jobs. Make sure that any jobs which are particularly relevant to the locality are included – perhaps there is an important local manufacturing industry, or a slightly unusual local shop.

All this done, give one of the 'occupation cards' to each child and put the children into pairs. Each child keeps the card secret from the other child and they take it in turns to ask questions of their partner to find out what that person's job is. Here are some questions they might ask:
▲ Is your job an indoor or an outdoor one?
▲ Is it a night or day job?

69

▲ Do you work with people/machines/animals?

▲ Do you wear special clothing for your job?

▲ What tools/equipment do you use?

This activity effectively introduces the children to the jobs in question and involves them in a careful consideration of them.

Give out copies of the photocopiable sheet and explain to the children that they are going to write a day's diary entry for someone doing the job on their card as though that person lives in the locality being studied.

Images and a map of the locality might assist the children in thinking of a typical working day for their person. Children should be encouraged to make the diary entry as real as possible by including references to place names, street names and other 'human' features of the locality (for example, they could mention going to the bank at lunchtime and where they went for lunch).

Suggestion(s) for extension

Children could be encouraged to include a map of their day's route.

Suggestion(s) for support

Consider the ability of individuals when distributing the 'job cards'. Some jobs are going to be easier to write about (for example, a teacher) than other, less known or more obscure occupations (such as a publisher).

Assessment opportunities

Examine completed diary entries to see whether a child has managed to include references to local places, features, road names, traditions (a child might include reference to traditional sources of employment – for example, the potteries in Stoke-on-Trent – or other traditions in the local area) and so on.

Opportunities for IT

The children could write their diaries using a word processor. If the activity is undertaken over a long period of time, the children should save their work so that they can retrieve and develop it at a later time. Children may need to be shown how to set up headings or hanging indents to format their diary.

Display ideas

Get the children to paint or draw large pictures of the characters they have adopted and the places where those characters would work in the locality being studied. Display the pictures so that each character, its place of work and its diary entry are grouped together.

Other aspects of the Geography PoS covered

1b; 3a, e; 5c.

Reference to photocopiable sheet

Photocopiable page 136 is for the children to write their diary entry. Each child imagines that they are a person living in the contrasting UK locality.

ENVIRONMENTAL ISSUES 'RADIO'

To explore and communicate an important environmental issue to others in a contrasting UK locality.

†† *Small groups within a class.*

🕐 *This activity lends itself to being carried out over two lessons – 10 minutes discussion; 40 minutes small group work/research; 30 minutes class 'studio' activity; (20 minutes listening activity – optional).*

Previous skills/knowledge needed

Children should have some understanding of what the term 'environment' means and what environmental issues tend to involve. They should already have some understanding of the contrasting locality being studied and they should be used to working with a tape recorder. Children will use their speaking and listening skills in this activity.

Key background information

During Key Stage 2 children should have opportunities to learn of real issues affecting a real place. The contrasting locality will become much more real to the children if a genuine issue in that locality can be studied. Children should learn about the human and physical processes which are operating in a place, and become aware of the problems, concerns, anxieties and challenges faced by real people.

Preparation

Acquaint yourself with an environmental issue which exists in the locality you are studying with the children. Arrange to have copies of a local newspaper mailed to your school for a short period.

Issues worth studying might surround:

▲ parking problems
▲ pollution problems
▲ traffic congestion problems
▲ loss of green land
▲ pressure on the land from tourists
▲ the 'up-grading' of a road

Choose an issue from the material you have collected and display source material so that the children will be able to view it.

Resources needed

Audio tape recorder (you may require a separate microphone) and suitable tape, source materials on an environmental issue from the contrasting locality you are studying (newspaper articles are very suitable), one copy of photocopiable page 137 (and 138, if necessary) per child.

What to do

Show the children the display of newspaper articles and ask them what they think is the linking theme. Discuss any similar issues in your own locality.

Discuss what makes an effective television programme (such as, interesting subject, varied style of presentation, varied locations, involvement of real people) and, based on this, lead the discussion into the added problems that a radio journalist has in making the places covered by a programme seem real (lack of visual presentation) and so on.

Tell the children that they are going to make a radio programme about the issue and get them to brainstorm the

71

programme's plan. The programme should include the sections on the their programme planning sheet (photocopiable page 137). An example has been done on photocopiable page 138. Use this to prompt the children if they become stuck.

Give each child a copy of photocopiable page 137. Divide the children up into writing groups and allocate each group one part of the programme to research. Each group writes its part of the programme in rough. They decide on how they are going to present their piece of work, who is going to read it and whether they need such things as sound effects. They then complete their section of the sheet. (This will mean that the same group will have the same information; however, they will be filling out the rest of the sheet on their own merits.)

The class then sit quietly around the tape recorder and a 'studio atmosphere' is adopted. The groups take it in turn to record their part of the programme. Once the whole programme has been recorded you can test the children's listening skills by getting them to listen to the finished programme, filling in the remaining sections of the photocopiable sheets with what they learn by listening.

Radio 'environment' Programme planning sheet 2

Date
Names of reporters/researchers.
Sally, Ahmed, Mark, Gemma

Where in the UK is the programme about?
Folkestone

Description of the area
Small, old town. Chalky cliffs. Lots of fields. Near to port of Dover.

What is the environmental issue?
Channel tunnel comes out here. Has caused lots of disagreement among locals. Loss of green land. More traffic.

Radio 'environment' Programme planning sheet 1

Date
Names of reporters/researchers

Where in the UK is the programme about?

Description of the area.

What is the environmental issue?

The main views people have on the issue.

Interviews.

How the issue might change the area.

Summary.

Suggestion(s) for extension
Children capable of doing so could research their part of the programme further than the information in the articles. They could telephone, fax or e-mail interested parties in the UK locality being studied.

Suggestion(s) for support
Group your children so that those requiring extra support are seated next to children with, for example, better reading skills. Children are often encouraged in this kind of work if they are told that theirs is the voice to be used in the completed piece of work.

Assessment opportunities
Before the children begin the last part of the activity, explain that you will be looking at their notes on the photocopiable sheet to see how much they have learned about the issue in the locality concerned.

Opportunities for IT
Some simple elements of control are involved in using tape recorders especially in editing their work.

The children could create a mutli-media presentation of the environmental issue of the locality using an authoring package. This could combine scanned maps of the locality, pictures from the local newspaper or other photographs. The tape recorded commentary could be added to the presentation using a microphone attached to the computer.

Display ideas
Display the articles from the newspaper(s) along with a map showing the locality being studied and copies of the children's planning sheets. The tape recorder could be positioned below the display. Connect it to a listening station with multiple headsets and write labels inviting the observers to listen to your class' programme.

Other aspects of the Geography PoS covered
1b; 2b,c; 3a, e; 5d; 9c.

Reference to photocopiable sheets
Photocopiable page 137 is used to help children plan their part of a 'radio' programme to be recorded by the whole class using an audio tape recorder. Children fill in the rest of the sheet while listening to the completed programme. Photocopiable page 138 can be used to prompt children who have difficulties.

GEOGRAPHY
KS2: PLACES

PEOPLE AND LOCALITIES IN THE UK

To appreciate the connection between the features of a contrasting UK locality and human activity within it.

†† *Individuals.*

🕐 *5–10 minutes introduction; 25 minutes mapping activity; 20 minutes worksheet activity.*

Previous skills/knowledge needed

Children should be capable of using tracing paper. They should have some experience of map interpretation.

Key background information

It is important that children recognise the connection between the existing physical and human components of landscape and human features and activities today.

▲ Canals follow contours because of the physical problems involved in them ascending hills.

▲ Coal mines have to locate over coal fields.

▲ Modern industrial activity locates in peripheral industrial parks because town residents object to lorries. The motorways needed by the lorries run past the edge of towns and not through their centres.

There are normally several reasons attributing to the location of human activity. These will include such things as:

▲ the shape of the land

▲ the location of other settlements in the area

▲ existing transport routes

▲ location of raw materials

▲ planning regulations.

Preparation

Make A4 copies of the 1:50 000 map of your contrasting UK locality and obtain a supply of A4 tracing paper. Prepare yourself by identifying the main communication routes in the locality and the major relief features (hills, valleys, rivers and so on).

Resources needed

A4 copies of the locality's 1:50 000 (Landranger) Ordnance Survey map, two pieces of A4 tracing paper and one copy of photocopiable page 139 for each child, coloured felt-tipped pens, pencils.

What to do

Distribute the map copies and ask the children to identify the rivers, lakes, valleys, hills and other physical features (these may include coastline features).

Once the children have done this tell them to lay one of their pieces of tracing paper over the top of the map and to trace, in pencil at first, the hills, valleys, rivers, cliffs and other physical features. There are a number of ways that they might do this. Some children will want to try to depict features in a plan view, others will want to draw and possibly even annotate.

Next get the children to repeat the exercise (using their second piece of tracing paper), this time tracing the main human features including:

▲ main roads and motorways

▲ railway lines

▲ major residential areas

▲ major industrial areas

▲ leisure facilities such as parks.

The children could devise a key for both their traced maps.

Give each child a copy of the photocopiable sheet and ask them to complete it showing each human feature or activity in the first column, physical features which may account for its location in the second column and existing human features which may have affected its location in the third.

Some children will find the interpretation of the photocopied version of the map very difficult. Grid lines and contour lines may well 'cloud' the map making it confusing. Consider highlighting important features on the children's photocopies (for example, marking any blue lines/rivers) or spending more time using a colour master copy at the outset.

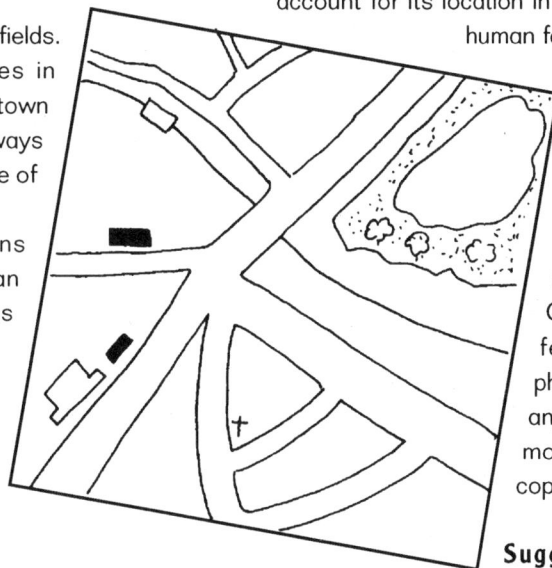

Suggestion(s) for extension

Some children will want to redraw the map showing the physical and human features they have identified. This should be encouraged.

Suggestion(s) for support

Some children will benefit from doing the first tracing, transferring features identified in this tracing to the photocopiable sheet, then doing the second tracing and finally transferring its features. This will help them to concentrate on whether they are looking at physical features or existing human features.

Assessment opportunities

The photocopiable sheet can offer an effective piece of evidence as to a child's ability to recognise cause and effect in the location of human features. Children should be able to identify some of the physical and/or human factors which account for the location of different human activities.

Opportunities for IT

Children can re-draw their simplified maps using the drawing package on a computer. Draw a template map yourself (containing simple dots as key points) and then ask each child to draw the human and physical features on saved copies of the base map.

Display ideas

Create a large wall display incorporating all of the original maps and the children's work or create two large maps side by side on a wall board, one showing the physical features of the contrasting locality and the other showing the human features. Get the children to make labels explaining specific links and to position them on the board with threads linking to the features they refer to.

Children could model the features identified in the photocopiable sheet lists and make a table top model display which incorporates human and physical features.

Other aspects of the Geography PoS covered

1b, c; 3a, c, d; 5a; 9b.

Reference to photocopiable sheet

Photocopiable page 139 provides a structure for children to record the way that physical features and existing human features affect human activities. Children identify a human feature or activity in the first column, identify any physical and existing human features that have affected its location in the second and third columns respectively.

CHANGES IN A UK LOCALITY

To understand some of the important changes operating in a contrasting UK locality.

†† *Individuals.*

🕐 *15 minutes discussion and examination of resources; 30 minutes photocopiable sheet activity.*

Previous skills/knowledge needed

Children should already have been introduced to the locality being studied. They should be able to draw in an imaginative context.

Key background information

A major component to understanding a contrasting locality is to recognise how that locality is changing. Children should know something of how it has changed in the recent past and how it is likely to change in the near future. You should draw children's attention to the change in building styles, the necessity for wider roads, the changes in the amounts of green areas in urban areas and the way in which levels of noise and other pollutants have altered.

Preparation

Enlarge a copy of photocopiable page 140 and collect as many pictures, books, maps and other resources about your contrasting locality as you can. The resources could form a stimulus display.

**GEOGRAPHY
KS2: PLACES**

Resources needed

A collection of pictures, books and maps about the contrasting UK locality, copy of photocopiable page 140 (enlarged), paper, coloured pencils.

What to do

Allow the children to examine the display of resource materials and the copy of the photocopiable sheet which can be used for initial discussion and explanation of what you want them to do. Ask them to draw a picture of a part of the contrasting locality you are studying. This picture might be taken directly from a picture in the display (not the photocopiable sheet) or might represent a 'typical' scene in the locality. Next ask the children to label the picture and write a *description* of the view.

Now ask the children to draw pictures of what they think the view would have looked like in the past and what they think it will look like in the future. The children label the years that they have tried to portray and write *explanations* of how they are different from their first picture.

They could organise their work either in the same format as photocopiable page 140, or, if they require more space, they could use a different sheet for each drawing.

Suggestion(s) for extension

More able children may work out detailed factual information about change in the locality from the resources you have supplied. If they can do this, encourage them to incorporate it in their drawings and writing.

Suggestion(s) for support

Some children will benefit from guidance at the stage where they choose an image for their first picture. The activity is easier if a child chooses a scene where the changes through time are clear.

Assessment opportunities

Ask each child to choose one factor which they think has changed from the past in the location they have depicted, and one factor they think is likely to change in the future. Get the children to tell the rest of the group about these changes and record whether each child has a reasonable understanding of how the locality has and is changing.

Opportunities for IT

Children could use an art or drawing package to create their first picture. If this is saved on to a disk they can then use this original as the basis for the pictures showing the past and future views. Older or more able children might be able to use a scanned photographic image as the basis for their past and future pictures. They will need to be shown how to select or mix colours to match those on the scanned image, and to cut and copy sections of the picture.

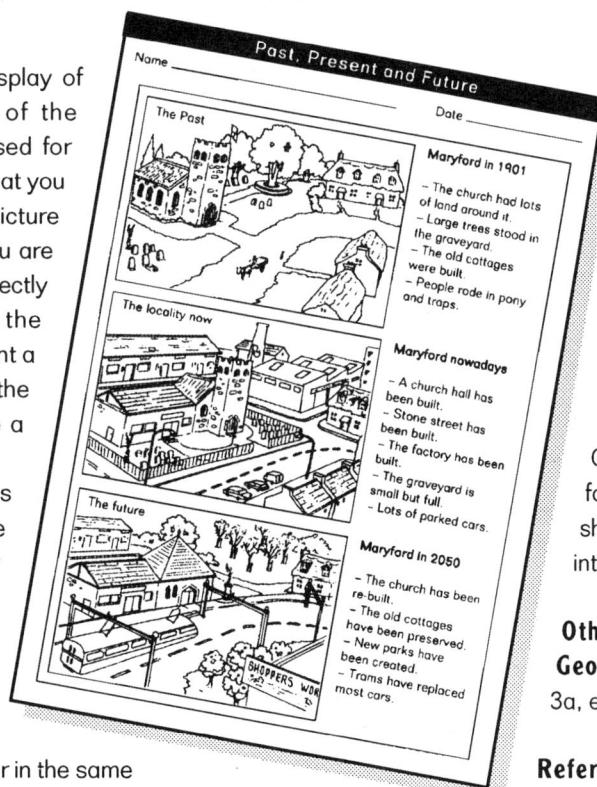

Display ideas

Display the resources you collected about the locality and the item's of children's work. Position the children's work near to any photographs or other images which it relates to. A three-part display could be made with the headings 'Past', 'Present' and 'Future' (if the work is the same format as the photocopiable sheet it will need to be cut up into the three groups).

Other aspects of the Geography PoS covered

3a, e; 5a; 10a.

Reference to photocopiable sheet

Photocopiable page 140 is used as a discussion focus to give the children an idea of what is expected of them. The sheet shows an imaginary town with views of what it might have looked like in the past above it and what it might look like in the future below it. Notes give the children ideas of the sorts of change which they might register for their own work.

PUTTING IT ON THE MAP

To be able to connect the contrasting UK locality with other parts of the British Isles using a map.

†† *Individuals in group/class.*

🕐 *10 minutes introduction; 30 minutes map activity.*

Previous skills/knowledge needed
Children should be able to use the index and contents pages of a UK road atlas.

Key background information
It is very important that children are able to put the contrasting locality being studied in context within the UK and that they should know where it is on the UK map. The location of the place you are studying should be known relative to other key settlements and communication routes of importance to it.

Preparation
Collect atlases with reasonably detailed maps of Britain and national road atlases. Parents are sometimes prepared to allow children to bring a road atlas into school if they are given enough notice.

Resources needed
A collection of atlases (see above), copies of photocopiable page 141 for each child, pencils, erasers.

What to do
Distribute the atlases and give each child a copy of the photocopiable page.

First, ask the children to draw a small dot on the map of the UK to show where they live. This done ask the children to use the index and contents pages to locate the following:
▲ the contrasting UK locality being studied;
▲ London, Edinburgh, Cardiff and Belfast;
▲ the nearest motorway(s) to the locality studied (its/their entire length);
▲ the settlements at each end of this/these motorway(s);
▲ the nearest railway line to the locality studied (and its links with major cities);
▲ the London, Edinburgh and Belfast station connecting with this line;
▲ the nearest administrative settlement to the locality ('county town/city');
▲ the most efficient route to this settlement by road;
▲ the nearest port and airport and connecting roads and railways between them and the locality;
▲ the boundary of the counties or regions containing your own and the contrasting locality;
▲ the roads and railway lines which connect your own locality to the contrasting locality being studied.

They should label these on their map in pencil – remembering that they may need to rub out and reposition the labels slightly due to detail being added later. On the same map, they would go on to do the same for any other UK localities that they have studied.

Suggestion(s) for extension
Children can go further than the list suggested here. They could mark features such as the nearest mountain, river, lake, canal, tourist resort, premier league football club. Involve the children in deciding on other places to be included.

Suggestion(s) for support
Problems are likely to be associated with transferring from page to page within atlases. You could provide children with

Connect them up

Name _____

Date _____

Key:
- ⊙ Capital
- • City/Town
- ○ Village
- ≡ Motorway
- ⊬ Railway
- ▬ Railway station
- — Road
- ⚓ Port
- ✗ Airport
- ⋯ County/Region boundary

THIS LOCALITY – THAT LOCALITY

To recognise the similarities and differences between the contrasting UK locality and your own locality.

†† *Individuals.*

🕐 *10 minutes introduction; 15 minutes land use mapping activity; 15 minutes photocopiable page mapping; 15 minutes table and graph activity; (15 minutes optional writing activity).*

Previous skills/knowledge needed
Children should be able to read large scale maps.

Key background information
The geographical skill of land use mapping is used here to highlight the similarities and differences between your locality and the contrasting UK locality that you study. It is an important and very graphic way of demonstrating such similarities and differences and necessarily relies on the children adopting a common key across both maps.

sticky 'memo labels' to mark the main pages they will need to refer to.

Assessment opportunities
Once a group of children have completed the basic activity give them a further ten minutes to study their maps and then collect the maps in. Provide each child with a new copy of the photocopiable sheet and ask them to mark each feature from memory as you read them out.

Opportunities for IT
The children could use a map taken from a clipart collection such as *Bitfolio* and load this into a drawing package. Children can use the text and drawing tools to label and mark the features on the map.

Display ideas
A group of children could enjoy recreating the map produced as a large wall map. Photocopy a blank map of the UK onto acetate and then project it on to the wall using an overhead projector. The children can draw around the coastline, add the borders and the details from their paper maps.

Other aspects of the Geography PoS covered
1a, d; 3c, d.

Reference to photocopiable sheet
Photocopiable page 141 is a blank map of the UK. Children add the places and features listed above and thus create a map which identifies the main links between the contrasting UK locality being studied and the rest of the country.

Preparation
Select large scale maps which show your own locality and the contrasting locality being studied. It is important that both these maps hold as much information about the locality as possible and it is very important that they are the same scale. Ordnance Survey 1:10 000 would be an appropriate scale.

Photocopy both maps and on a copy of each, draw a 10cm × 10cm square centred on the point of greatest relevance to your studies. Cut these two squares out and

stick them one beside the other on a sheet of A4. Now photocopy this sheet and photocopiable pages 142 and 143, one for each child.

Resources needed
Map sheets (as explained above) and copies of photocopiable pages 142 and 143 for each child, a selection of pencil crayons, rulers.

What to do
Distribute the map sheets and copies of the photocopiable sheets 142 and 143 to the children and explain that they should start with the square showing their own locality and colour the map in with pencil crayon according to this key (as included on sheet 142):

▲ residential	blue
▲ shopping	red
▲ industrial/commercial	brown
▲ agricultural	green
▲ leisure facilities	pink
▲ educational	yellow
▲ medical	orange
▲ places of worship (land/buildings)	purple
▲ transport/communication	grey
▲ other	white

This done, ask the children to repeat the activity using the map square for the contrasting locality.

Now explain to the children that they have to colour in the grids on sheet 142, the left grid relating to the school's locality and the right one relating to the contrasting locality. They may wish to draw their own grids with rulers, over the map extracts to help them (alternatively, the teacher could photocopy sheet 142 on to acetate so that the child can superimpose a transparent grid over the original map).

For each 1cm² they decide on the predominant colour on the extract map and transfer this colour to their grids.

Once they have done this for both map extracts, the children fill in the percentage tables on sheet 143 to show the percentages (each 1cm² square being 1% of the overall grid) for each land use type. The children can now graph the information using the axes provided on sheet 143.

In conclusion the children should be asked to write an interpretation of the two graphs which focuses on the similarities and differences between the two localities.

Suggestion(s) for extension
Some children may feel over constrained by having to designate one land use type only to each 1cm² square. Suggest that they draw a faint diagonal line across each square and use two colours per square where it is appropriate. They will then have to count each half square as 0.5% of the total for the percentage tables.

Suggestion(s) for support
Some children will find the interpretation of the contrasting locality map extract difficult as they may not have the knowledge provided by a visit to the place. Provide as much in the way of picture resource material to help these children determine land use.

Assessment opportunities
Assess the children's completed photocopiable sheets 142 and 143 and their written interpretations of their graphs to determine whether they have an understanding of the similarities and differences between the two localities.

Opportunities for IT
The children can create their own tables and graphs using a data handling, spreadsheet or graphing program on the computer. Children should be able to print out effective and colourful finished graphs and could even word process their final written interpretation.

Display ideas
Each child will enjoy mounting his own map sheet, grid sheet, graph sheet and written interpretation on to a large piece of sugar paper. Alternatively a large, whole class version of this could be created by the children to make a colourful wall display.

Other aspects of the Geography PoS covered
1a, b, c; 2c; 3d; 5a.

What's the difference?

Are they the same?

THEMATIC STUDIES AND OUR UK LOCALITY

To create an information bank about your own locality.

Four groups.

5 minutes introduction; 30 minutes research and photocopiable sheet activity.

Previous skills/knowledge needed
Children should be able to examine and extract information from a range of resources.

Key background information
A data sheet is simply a method of collecting and organising information so that it can be used in a meaningful way.

The data sheet is used here for the children to compile a data bank on the subjects of 'Rivers', 'Weather', 'Settlements' and 'Environment' for the contrasting UK locality being studied.

Preparation
Gather together a selection of information on the contrasting locality you are studying. Make this as wide a range of information as you can. It might include books, pictures, leaflets, maps and artefacts, and collected items such as stones, fir cones and sand.

Make copies of photocopiable pages 144 and 145 and four 'table' labels, one for each of the four Key Stage 2 themes (as mentioned in 'Key background information').

Resources needed
Resources on the locality (see above), four table labels and copies of photocopiable pages 144 and 145 for each child.

What to do
Place each label on a separate table so that there is a table for each of the four themes. Spread the resources around the four tables in a random fashion.

Reference to photocopiable sheets
Photocopiable page 142 is used to transfer information from colour coded land use maps already completed by the children according to the key at the bottom of the sheet. Children decide on the most appropriate colour for each 1cm².

Photocopiable page 143 is used to make land use percentage tables for the two localities and then to graph the information.

79

Provide each child with copies of the photocopiable sheets and tell them that they have to collect the information asked for. This information asked involves them in:

▲ finding places (for example, the nearest station);
▲ finding information on places (for example, what is the name of the school?);
▲ finding information calculated using the map (for example, distance from the nearest town).

The children are separated into four groups and told that they are to move from table to table in a 'rotating group' fashion. Explain that as they visit each table they should try to fill in the part of their sheets which relate to that table's title. Tell them that if they come across a piece of information which is particularly relevant to one of the tables they should move it to that table. As the activity unfolds, therefore, the resources should sort themselves making the collection of information easier. Emphasise accuracy with the children in the filling in of their data collection sheets.

Each child should end up with a collection of information on the four themes and information on where they found the information.

Suggestion(s) for extension

Encourage children who want to add questions (and find the answers) to the four (theme) sections on photocopiable sheets 144 and 145. They could extend their work on to a separate piece of paper.

Suggestion(s) for support

Some children will find the task of locating the required information a difficult one and may be effectively paired with more able children. Reading ability might be a key basis for this pairing.

Assessment opportunities

It is inappropriate to assess the children's understanding of the four geographical themes from this activity but you could make an effective evaluation of their abilities of gathering information as referred to in section 2 of the Programme of Study.

Opportunities for IT

This activity can translate very well into using the spreadsheet application of your computer. Type the categories and questions into a column of cells on the left of a spreadsheet page and save the file as a template. The children can then open copies of this template and input the information accordingly.

CD-ROM atlases, locality packs and encyclopaedia can offer much as resource bases on many UK localities.

Display ideas

Make a display using the materials you collected to stimulate the children. These could be displayed on a table top and children's completed work displayed around the table.

Other aspects of the Geography PoS covered

1b; 2a–c; 3a, d, e; 5a; 6–10.

Reference to photocopiable sheets

Photocopiable pages 144 and 145 are used to collect a range of information about the contrasting UK locality being studied. Children also record where they found the information.

**GEOGRAPHY
KS2: PLACES**

Studying a contrasting overseas locality

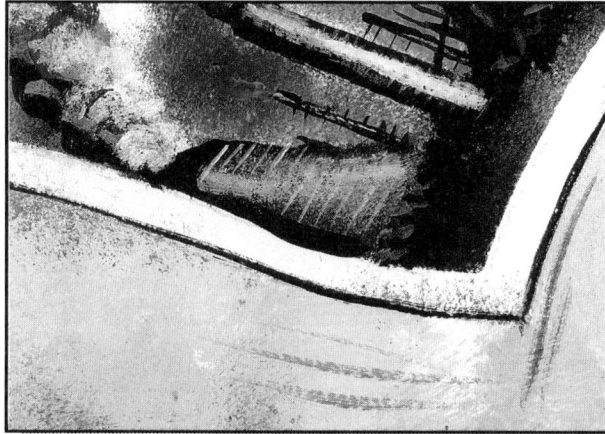

The National Curriculum stipulates that the contrasting overseas locality:

'...should be in Africa, Asia (excluding Japan), South America or Central America (including the Caribbean)'. (DfE, 1995)

This is important to consider when choosing where to study as your contrasting overseas locality. Children should learn of other parts of the world when studying the themes of rivers, weather, settlement and environmental change and it is particularly important to provide the children with an overview which puts places being studied in a world as well as a locational context.

The aim is for them to gain an understanding of what it would really be like to live in that place and to do that they must gain a fairly intimate knowledge of it, its inhabitants, issues in that place and how it is changing. Children should learn of its weather characteristics, its physical features (is it a mountainous area?), its human features (is it urban, suburban or rural? what land use types are there? how does the human environment reflect the way that people spend their time?), and how it is linked to other places.

Choose the locality that you study with great care and ensure that comparisons can be made with your own locality and the contrasting UK locality that the children will study. It is inevitably the case that overseas localities will be studied through secondary sources and it is the job of the teacher to prepare as wide a variation and as high a quality of resources about the locality as is possible.

ALL AROUND THE WORLD

To be able to put places studied in the course of their school work into a world context.

†† *Pairs within groups. Four groups in all.*

🕐 *10 minutes group work/discussion; 20–30 minutes paired research work; 10 minutes group work.*

Previous skills/knowledge needed

Children should be used to using the index and contents pages of a world atlas and should be acquainted with a world map and a globe. They should be used to collaborative working and using the school library area.

Key background information

It is very important that as children encounter places in their school work and their own family experiences by visiting them or indirectly through such media as books or television, that they should be able to place each one in a wider, world context.

Children should always have access to a world map, a globe and appropriate world atlases and they should also be given opportunities to improve their abilities at using reference materials and their library skills.

Children will learn about a range of places in their schooling but they will not necessarily learn how all of these places are linked to the rest of the world and specifically to their own home area. An interrogation sheet, which children can use with respect to any place in the world that they might encounter, allows the children to focus on putting places they come across into a world context.

Preparation

Prepare a part of your classroom as a 'places' area. Display a world map, a globe, atlases and non-fiction books on as wide a range of places as you can. Ensure that children can have access to any library area where non-fiction or topic books are kept. Photocopy page 146 for each child.

Resources needed

A world map, globe, atlases and books as referred to above. Copies of photocopiable page 146 for each child. Use of the school library area.

What to do

Divide the children into four groups and allocate a part of the world to each group. This is best done by dividing the world map and globe into four by marking a line along the equator and a line down the prime meridian (and down the line of 180° longitude on the globe).

Challenge pairs of children within each group to find information from the source material about four places in their sector of the world. The photocopiable sheet involves the children in researching the following:

▲ name of the place
▲ name of its continent
▲ name of its country
▲ city, town or village
▲ coastal or inland
▲ climate details
▲ landscape details
▲ language(s) spoken
▲ ways people make a living.

Tell the children that they are going to be using their research skills and that they might have to visit the school library area. Allow each group some time to sit around a table and pool ideas for places in their sector of which they may already know something. Encourage the children to research places that they have heard of in the news, on television, from books or from school work. Some of them may even have been to places in their sector.

Each pair of children uses the source materials to research four places in their sector and fills in the photocopiable page with information on two places each. It will be a very interesting and worthwhile exercise to involve the children in sharing their findings with each other. This could even be organised into a fun quiz.

Suggestion(s) for extension

Children may wish to develop further categories to research. One possible additional heading might be 'typical food eaten'. The photocopiable sheet could be used for this purpose, using the blank spaces provided.

Suggestion(s) for support

Limit the number of category headings you require the children to research. You could prepare the activity more precisely by gathering books on the four sectors to save the children time in seeking information.

Assessment opportunities

It is possible to make a general assessment of a child's understanding of the world as a whole by monitoring a targeted child and assessing whether that child can consistently apply the relevant information for each category (for example, does the child consistently recognise the difference between country and continent).

Opportunities for IT

The children could use CD-ROM resources for research which might include encyclopaedia, atlases, world databases and picture collections. If the school has Internet access they could use the World Wide Web to locate information on different places.

Display ideas

Use the 'places' area in your classroom as a stimulus area for this activity. One copy of photocopiable sheet from each group could be displayed around the world map, with threads connecting the places referred to on the sheets to their locations on the map.

Other aspects of the Geography PoS covered

1a, b, d; 3a, d, e.

Reference to photocopiable sheet

Photocopiable page 146 is used by the children to record information gathered about places in the sector of the world that you have allocated to their group. There is room on each sheet for the children to document two places using the headings provided. As the children are working in pairs, they will be able to research four places between them.

LAND AND SEA

To consolidate knowledge of some of the world's major physical features. To put contrasting overseas localities studied into a world context.

†† *Individuals/pairs.*

🕐 *5 minutes introduction; 15–20 minutes photocopiable sheet activity.*

Previous skills/knowledge needed

Children should have studied or be studying a contrasting locality overseas. They should be capable of using colour to shade maps. They should be able to use the index and contents pages of a world atlas and be capable of operating a map key.

Key background information

It is important that children begin to develop an awareness of the physical variations and extremes (with reference to areas of water and land) which exist in the world as a whole, as well as the physical features (and conditions) operating in the specific parts of the world which they study. They should be able to put both their own home region and contrasting overseas localities into an overall world context.

A physical map of the world will be useful for this activity. Such a map tends to show the land area primarily in greens and browns or yellows (deserts), and areas of water in blues (sea, lakes). White is often used to depict permanent ice while shades of purple reflect areas of high altitude. Different shades of greens and blues are used to reflect variations in vegetation and different depths of sea. This is opposed to a human or political map which shows the world as a 'patchwork quilt' of coloured countries. (On the photocopiable sheet the key has been simplified to help the children.)

Preparation
Display a physical map of the world so that all the children can see it. Copy photocopiable page 147 for each child.

Resources needed
A physical world map, a world atlas per pair of children, pencil crayons (blue, green, brown and yellow), copies of photocopiable page 147 for each child.

What to do
Provide each child with a copy of photocopiable page 147. Each child shares an atlas with a partner and uses it to help locate the features listed on the photocopiable sheet. They then find each of the features on the map and colour them on the photocopiable sheet with the appropriate colour according to the key at the bottom. They write the appropriate number in each box according to the key on the left.

This map can be used as a reference map when studying contrasting overseas localities.

Suggestion(s) for extension
Some children might be encouraged to take the activity further by identifying additional areas of mountains, deserts and forests, and permanently frozen areas. They could mark additional major world rivers as well. You could enlarge copies of the photocopiable sheet for children who choose to go into some detail.

Suggestion(s) for support
Pair children so that more able readers support less able ones. This will assist children in their use of reference pages in atlases.

Assessment opportunities
Use the photocopiable sheet to assess whether, given the use of an atlas and world map, a child is capable of recognising some of the main physical features of the world.

Opportunities for IT
There are a range of CD-ROM encyclopaedia, atlas and other world data programs available including some excellent ones covering the physical world. Children could interrogate such programs to find the information they need.

Display ideas
Create a wall display using a large (say A1) class produced map of the world with the features covered by this activity marked on it. If you produce the outline map (a good way of doing this is to photocopy page 147 on to acetate, project it on to a large piece of white paper and then draw around the outline), the children could take it in turns to colour in the physical features. Alternatively, they could cut out the features from coloured paper and layer them if necessary.

Other aspects of the Geography PoS covered
1a, d; 3a, c, d, e.

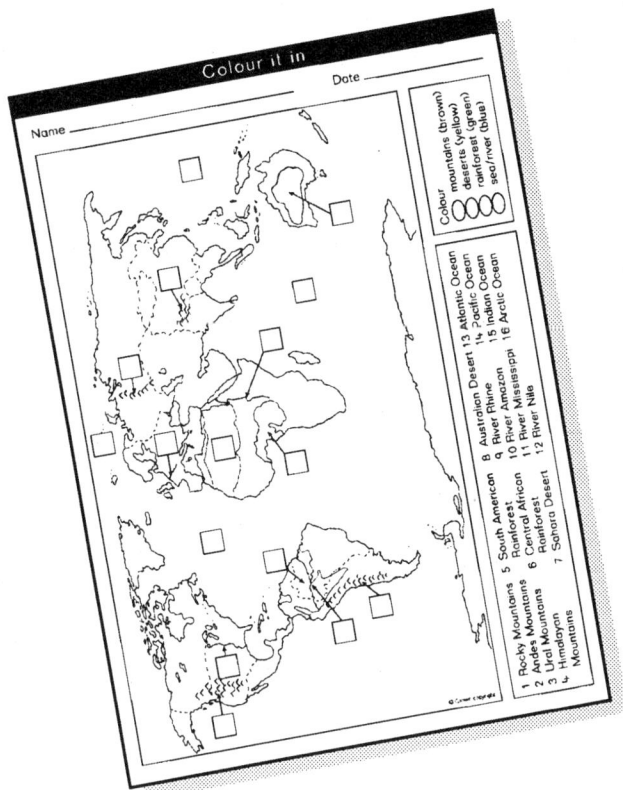

Colour it in

Name _____ Date _____

Colour
mountains (brown)
deserts (yellow)
rainforest (green)
sea/river (blue)

1 Rocky Mountains   5 South American   8 Australian Desert   13 Atlantic Ocean
2 Andes Mountains   Rainforest   9 River Rhine   14 Pacific Ocean
3 Ural Mountains   6 Central African   10 River Amazon   15 Indian Ocean
4 Himalayan   Rainforest   11 River Mississippi   16 Arctic Ocean
  Mountains   7 Sahara Desert   12 River Nile

SETTLEMENT SKYLINES

To compare features in your own settlement and a contrasting overseas settlement.

†† *Groups.*

🕐 *20 minutes group introduction; 40 minutes cutting, sticking and writing activities.*

Previous skills/knowledge needed

Children should have completed work on their own settlement and should have been introduced to a contrasting overseas settlement. They will need to be accurate in their cutting out skills.

Key background information

As an important part of children's learning about their world they should be involved in comparing and contrasting different places. Having gained a fairly intimate knowledge of their own locality they should be able to note the similarities and differences between that settlement and contrasting settlements overseas.

There are quite subtle differences between settlements as well as obvious ones, such as settlement size. The skyline of a settlement can be very impressive, like that of London or New York, or it can be more subtle in its characteristics, like that of a north African village or town with its flat roofs and occasional domed buildings. Trees and relief features such as hillsides also may form part of the skyline.

Reference to photocopiable sheet

Photocopiable page 147 is a map of the world with some of the world's most important features outlined (and as specified in the National Curriculum). The children work down the list of features at the bottom of the sheet and attribute the correct number to the correct box on the map. They use the colour key at the bottom of the sheet to colour in the map's features identifying rivers, mountain ranges, deserts, forest regions and oceans.

Preparation

Collect a variety of magazine pictures which show skylines (that is they include the line between sky and whatever is on the ground). Cut along the skylines on each of these pictures.

Gather together as many picture, video or computer generated resources as possible which show the built environment of both your own and the contrasting overseas localities you are studying.

Obtain an overhead projector. Copy photocopiable sheet 148 and carefully cut out the three skylines.

Resources needed

Your cut-outs of skylines (as above), an overhead projector, two sheets of trimmed black sugar paper for each child, pencils (or white crayons), scissors, glue and the cut-outs from photocopiable page 148.

What to do

Seat the children so that they can see the overhead projector and project each of the magazine cut-outs you have prepared. The magazine grade paper should completely obscure the light so that you are left with a silhouette of the skyline.

Involve the children in guessing which parts of the skylines are which and in making intelligent guesses as to what 'type' of settlement the skyline shows. Ask questions like:

**GEOGRAPHY
KS2: PLACES**

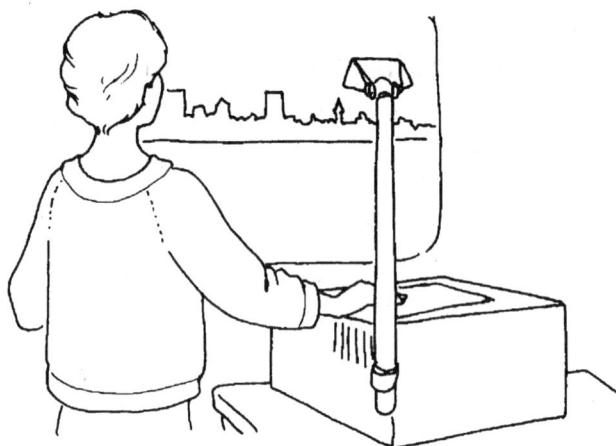

▲ is this place a large or a small settlement?

▲ is it urban or rural?

▲ is it in the UK, if so can they guess where?

▲ is it overseas, if so can they guess where?

▲ can they identify any specific features, for example a church spire?

Now project the three skylines that you have cut from the photocopiable sheet and discuss the sorts of places the children think they might portray. The first shows a UK country village, the second a town in north Africa and the third a town in south east Asia.

Now show the range of picture resources on the localities you are studying and discuss the features which might contribute to the skyline. Encourage the children to recognise that certain features give a skyline a characteristic or even unique 'feel'.

Give each child two pieces of the trimmed black sugar paper. Explain that they have to draw characteristic miniature skylines on to their pieces of sugar paper so that they accurately represent each of the two localities being studied. They should give some thought to this and will probably need to experiment in rough so as to end up with characteristic skylines.

Once the children have drawn their two skylines, they cut along the skyline and then they could write their descriptions of them and challenge friends to match their descriptions to the correct skyline.

Suggestion(s) for extension

Encourage those capable to include as great a degree of detail as they can. You could specifically challenge these children to include certain more complicated or unusual features.

Skylines

Suggestion(s) for support

Some children will find it easier to draw a picture of each of the places, cut along the skyline, put the bottom half on to a piece of the black paper, draw along the skyline edge of their original drawing and then cut out the final sugar paper skyline.

Children might be helped if you supply them with a list of likely 'skyline' words such as:

▲ spire

▲ roof

▲ tree

▲ tower

▲ aerial

▲ dome

▲ minaret

▲ crenellations

▲ castellations

Assessment opportunities

Use the idea of the children writing a description of their skylines (see end of 'What to do') and assess to what extent each child has an understanding of the specific characteristics that each of the localities have.

Opportunities for IT

Set up a template file for each child in a drawing program which has two boxes. Ask the children to draw a continuous skyline using the line drawing tools from one side of the box to the other.

Display ideas

A very effective wall display can be created by making two large scale versions of skylines using large (say A1) sheets of black sugar paper. Labelling could invite children to guess which skyline matches which place name. A table below the display could contain books and other resources which might help viewers of the display find the answers.

Other aspects of the Geography PoS covered

3e; 5b; 9a.

Reference to photocopiable sheet

Photocopiable page 148 is used by the teacher to focus discussion on different skylines. The teacher cuts out the three skylines prior to the lesson and projects their silhouettes using an overhead projector.

ENVIRONMENTAL DEBATE

To recognise that there are important environmental issues for people living in a contrasting overseas locality.

†† *Whole class in four groups.*

🕐 *10 minutes introduction; 60–75 minutes class debate.*

Previous skills/knowledge needed

Children should be used to working collaboratively and to the idea of going into role.

Decide on four major lines of argument with respect to the issue. An example might be as follows:

> The local government in a region in India wishes to build a new road through an area of agricultural land. The four 'interested parties' are:
> ▲ a government official supporting the road scheme;
> ▲ an official from a tea plantation which will benefit from improved communications;
> ▲ a local village official whose village will have to be relocated to make way for the road;
> ▲ a local farmer who will lose farmland because of the road.

Key background information

It is important that children recognise that real people live in the overseas localities which they study and that there are real issues operating in their lives. Role-play within an educational drama context is an excellent way of doing this.

A role-play 'public enquiry' debate is effective not only in airing real issues with the children but also in helping them to see that there are always 'two sides to the argument'.

The parts of the world from which the Key Stage 2 contrasting overseas locality can be taken tend to have very important development issues (issues surrounding the transition towards a high standard of living, economic prosperity and individual freedom). Such issues can be explored with young children and might include the roles of large multi-national companies, the plight of indigenous peoples, the destruction and mis-management of natural environments and unequal access to resources. Your nearest *Development Education Centre (DEC)* will be able to help you find resources and information.

Preparation

Decide on a real life issue which is of importance in the locality you are studying. You might glean such information from teaching materials about the locality or by obtaining news reports on the locality from newspapers, television, radio or the Internet.

This issue is provided for discussion purposes on photocopiable page 149.

Copy or group together any resources you have which support each of the four arguments surrounding your chosen issue. Write the names of the four interested parties on some paper (use photocopiable page 149 as an example) and copy this to give to the children.

Resources needed

Information materials as referred to above and five desk top place labels, four of them labelled with the name of one of each of the 'interested parties' in your debate and the fifth labelled 'chairperson'. Copies of photocopiable page 149 your prepared debate sheet for each child, pencils, paper.

What to do

Provide the children with copies of photocopiable page 149. Discuss the issue covered by the sheet (as in 'Preparation') and work through the four examples of people interested in the new road scheme. Get each child to write their understanding of what each of the four views are on a separate sheet of paper. Tell them that they should highlight the main disagreements between different parties. Discuss the children's work.

Put the children into four groups such that the overall ability of each group is comparable. Choose one child to act

GEOGRAPHY
KS2: PLACES

adult's help to maintain the necessary level of seriousness.

Assessment opportunities
Completed sheets will provide evidence of whether individual children have understood at least one side of the argument in the issue being studied.

Opportunities for IT
If your school is linked to the Internet, children could be involved in gathering information on the issue in question. Children could use a word processor program to present their main arguments which you could then photocopy on to acetate for them to present in the debate, using an overhead projector.

Display ideas
Create a display of the findings of each of the 'enquiry' groups with one part of the display for each of the main arguments. Incorporate the source materials used.

Other aspects of the Geography PoS covered
1b; 2c; 3a–e; 5d.

Reference to photocopiable sheets
Photocopiable page 149 is used to introduce the idea of different parties having different views on a real world issue. The issue of a new road threatening farming land and a village is presented and children are encouraged to re-write the main arguments and differences of opinion. This sheet can be used to design your own debate sheet.

as the impartial chairperson for the debate (or it may be necessary for you to act as the 'chair'). Position each group so that they are sitting together and then explain to all of the children that you are going to read them some material about the place you are studying.

Read the materials through once and then tell each group which 'interested party' they are going to be in the role-play debate.

Provide the children with copies of the debate sheet and explain that they are to listen very hard as you read through the materials again. Having done this, the children get together as a group and, using their notes, decide on the six main arguments which support their case. They should write these on their debate sheet.

Three children are then nominated from each of the groups to present their group's case in the debate. The first comes to the front and presents the group's six points to the rest of the class, each group's representative doing this in turn. The second representative from each group then comes to the front to respond to questions from the rest of the class which are asked 'through the chair'. Each group then gets back together and decides on a final two key points which they think are the most important for their case. You now ask all of the children except the third of each of the group's representatives to come out of role. The third representative comes to the front and presents these final points.

While the debate is going on and/or after the debate, get the children to fill in the rest of their debate sheet with their understanding of all the arguments. The 'dummy-run' with photocopiable page 149 should help them to understand what to do.

The chairperson now administers a vote on the issue.

Suggestion(s) for extension
Children could be asked to present a written portfolio of evidence to support their argument and they could even display this at the 'enquiry'.

Suggestion(s) for support
For a debate like this to work well, children have to be prepared to work in role. It is worth arranging a supporting

PLACE MODELS

To recognise the relationship between physical and human features in a contrasting overseas locality.

†† *Groups.*

🕐 *10 minutes introduction; 45 minutes modelling; (1 day's interval); 45 minutes modelling; 15 minutes reporting to rest of class.*

Previous skills/knowledge needed
Experience in using papier mâché and other materials in modelling will be an advantage. Children will need to work collaboratively.

Key background information
The physical terrain affects the human environment through such factors as slope, aspect (which way a slope faces) and appropriateness of the ground for building on. Steep slopes and poor soils or rocks are difficult to build on if the building is to have sound foundations. Also, if ground is low lying and prone to flooding there are obvious hazards to buildings. Children should be able to relate the human built environment to these physical factors.

Preparation
Gather old newspapers to use for papier mâché work and prepare paste. Gather a selection of small reclaimed materials modelling boxes. You will need a base board for the children to build the model on, ideally of approximately 1m square. Collect as many maps and photographs of the locality as you can. Display one large scale map of the locality with a square clearly marking a study area for this exercise. Protect the working area and the children's clothes as you would normally for art activities.

Resources needed
Maps and photographs of the contrasting locality, a base board of approximately 1m² and a supply of old newspapers, small reclaimed materials modelling boxes, paste and paint.

What to do
Show the children the map with the study area marked on it and help them to recognise what the map shows. Allow the group some time to look at the other picture and map resources you have provided and to locate where the views shown are on the main map.

Half of the group use papier mâché to build up a model of the shape of the ground in the square chosen for study, using the square base board. Using as many clues as possible from the pictures and the maps they show where any slopes and major landscape features are.

This will take the children some time. Once they have finished building the model up with newspaper they cover it with plain paper so that once it has dried it will be easy to paint.

While half of the group are doing this, the other half make models of the major buildings that are shown on the map (using photographic resources, if required). This is best done using small, thin card boxes similar to those in which drawing pins and paper-clips are supplied. Once the children have modelled the buildings they can write labels saying what each building is and then stick these on the buildings' roofs.

Having completed these tasks, and once the model has had a day or so to dry, half of the group can paint the model as it stands, putting on features like rivers, and the other half can begin to position and eventually stick the box buildings in their places on the model.

The class will end up with a model which shows both the locality's relief (shape of the land) and where its buildings are located.

Now ask the children to think about whether there is any relationship between where buildings are, which way they face and their design, and the physical ground on which they are built.

Give the children small slips of paper and ask them to write down one way in which the built environment results from the physical environment. These can then be mounted and displayed around the model.

Suggestion(s) for extension
Some children will be able to go into some detail, particularly with the buildings. Encourage children to look at which side of buildings the doorways are, how roofs are pitched, whether buildings rely on proximity to a water source and so on.

Suggestion(s) for support
The larger scale the original map, and therefore the smaller the area covered and the larger the individual features and buildings, the easier the activity will be for less able children. Also, the smaller the group, the easier children will find it to work together.

Assessment opportunities
Once the model is finished, get the children to explain the relationships between the built environment and the physical terrain and note whether individuals can demonstrate understanding of the relationships.

Opportunities for IT
Children can write simple labels for their models using the computer's word processor application.

Display ideas
The model will make an excellent table top display and can be positioned with the source materials, the base map and the children's strips of paper on the wall behind.

Others aspects of the Geography PoS covered
3c, d, e; 5a; 9b.

CONNECTIONS

To demonstrate an understanding of the communication links between the overseas locality being studied and your own locality.

†† *Individuals within a group.*

🕐 *5 minutes discussion; 30 minutes photocopiable sheet activity.*

Key background information
When studying overseas localities, children should not only gain a detailed knowledge of the locality itself but how that locality 'fits in' with the rest of the world. A knowledge of how the locality does this will help the children to understand why it is like it is and will also help the children develop a locational framework in which their own and this other locality can be positioned.

Primary school atlases vary in the detail on transport routes that they contain. Some have shipping, air, road and rail routes while others provide very little. If your atlases do not contain the information required, you may wish to provide additional resources for this activity.

Preparation
Make copies of photocopiable page 150 for each child and provide atlases.

Resources needed
A supply of atlases and other maps, pencil crayons, paper and a copy of photocopiable page 150 for each child.

What to do

Give each child a copy of photocopiable page 150 and explain that they have to mark on the place that they are studying.

Discuss the other places marked on the map and see if the children can find them in their atlases. If the atlases you are using contain thematic maps which show transport routes, then bring these to the children's attention.

Explain to the children that they have to choose three of the major world cities marked on the map and that they have to use their atlas to help them mark likely routes between the place being studied as a contrasting overseas locality and these places. One of these places should be London (the children could also mark their own locality in the British Isles).

The children are likely to mark roads, railways, air and sea routes and should do so using different colours for different transport types. Finally the sheet asks the children to design a key and this should reflect the different transport types with reference to the different colours they used for each. They should do this on a separate sheet of paper.

Suggestion(s) for extension

Encourage children to think of journeys which will use a range of transport types. For example, a journey to a Greek island could involve: travel by car or train to the airport, aeroplane to the mainland, boat to the island and taxi or walk to the location.

Suggestions(s) for support

Some children will find the scaling down of the atlas maps and the reference from one page to another difficult. Try to provide these children with a simpler, smaller scale, single sheet base map of the world; this should help them to navigate around the atlas.

Assessment opportunities

Examine the children's completed sheets to see whether they have shown realistic and reasonably accurately mapped routes. For example, have they included air routes between places where there are airports?

Opportunities for IT

The children could use a drawing package for this work. The task will be made easier if a pre-drawn map is used or one is taken from a clipart map collection. The children can then focus on the route rather than drawing the map. They could add labels of the ports or main towns on the route.

Children also could use a word processor to write a route guide to accompany the map. This could give directions to the main travel points and even information about the places passed through. The map and the guide could be presented together using a desktop publishing package.

Other aspects of the Geography PoS covered

1a, d; 3c, d.

Reference to photocopiable sheet

Photocopiable page 150 is central to this activity and shows a map of the world with various cities marked on it. This sheet could be enlarged which would make the children's work clearer.

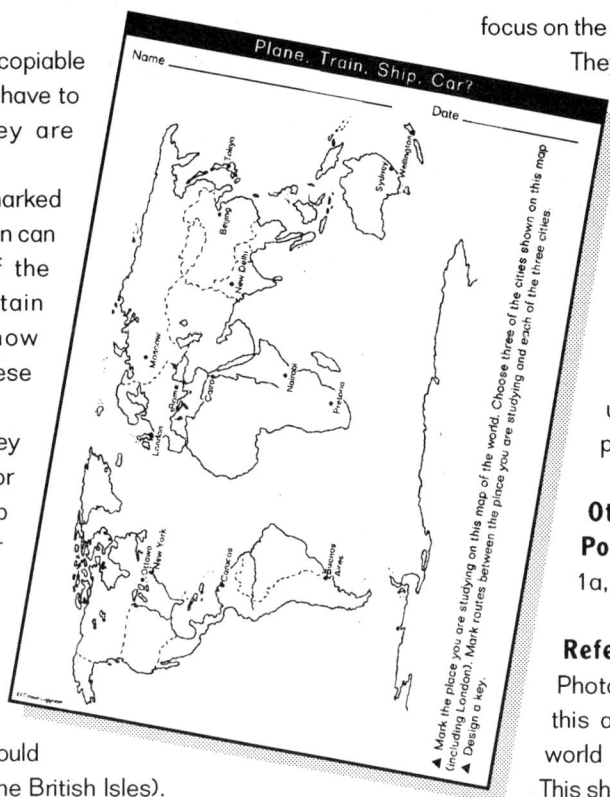

TWINS

To consider similarities and differences between your locality and a contrasting overseas locality.

†† *Whole class.*

🕐 *10 minutes discussion; 30 minutes photocopiable activity; 10 minutes 'voting' and discussion; (optional 60 minutes follow-up activity).*

Key background information

Most towns, cities and even villages have a coat of arms or some sort of symbol to represent them. The best coats of arms have component parts to their designs which sum up important human or physical features, or traditions of those places. Good symbols are representational, bold and clear.

Twinning (the development of a relationship between two or more towns or schools) can provide a very real and meaningful way of teaching children about real people in real places. Children can actually communicate with each other (by letter, telephone, fax, e-mail, the Internet or even visits) and can provide each other with useful and genuinely interesting data about their place.

Preparation

Collect together picture resources of the two places being studied and make a wall display with one half showing images of the children's own locality and the other half showing images of the contrasting locality.

Resources needed

Copy of photocopiable page 151 for each child, drawing pencils and other drawing materials. Picture resources for the stimulus display.

What to do

Show the children your display of picture images. Involve them in a discussion about the two localities. Discuss what human and physical features are similar or different, how aspects of people's lives compare and get the children to explain these similarities and differences.

Ask each child to select one image of each locality which they think really 'sums the area up', or represents the area well. Go around the class and ask each child to justify their choice.

Give each child a copy of photocopiable page 151 and explain that they are to form the committee which will design a joint coat of arms or 'logo' for a new twinning relationship between the two places.

The first coat of arms represents their own locality and the second coat of arms represents the contrasting locality.

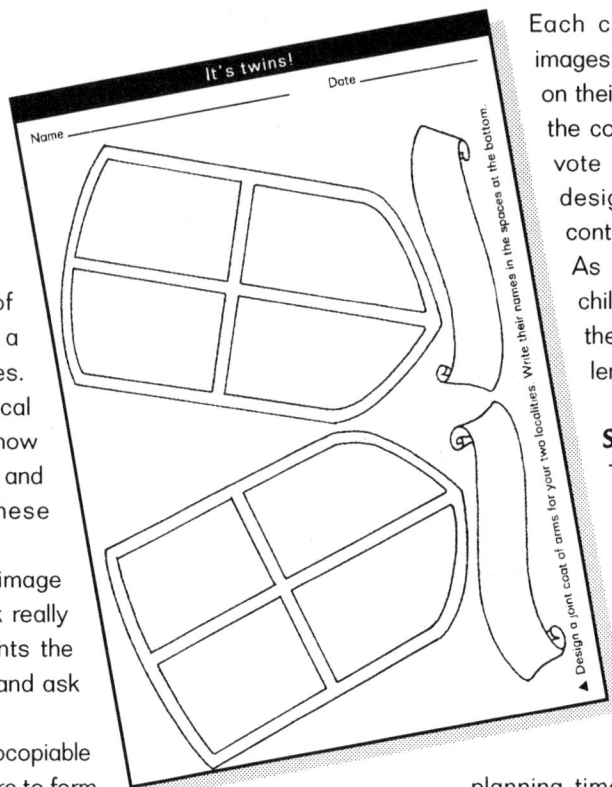

Each child chooses four important images for each shield and designs them on their sheet. This done, display all of the completed sheets and organise a vote on which of the home locality designs is best and which of the contrasting locality designs is best. As a follow-on activity a group of children can make a large version of the winning coats of arms. Collage lends itself to this type of activity.

Suggestion(s) for extension

To extend their understanding of the similarities and differences between the two localities you could ask those more able children to write a justification of their image choices.

Suggestion(s) for support

Provide children with more planning time or spend time at the outset actually picking out features as a group and sharing ideas about modifying them to make them suitable for this purpose.

Assessment opportunities

This activity can lead into an assessment of children's understanding of the similarities and differences between the localities. A written justification and explanation of the children's designs could be used as evidence or the discussion at the beginning of the activity could be used.

Opportunities for IT

The children could undertake this work using an art or drawing package. To make it easier a shield template can be created in advance and saved to disk. Each child can retrieve this file and use the drawing tools to draw and colour their design.

Display ideas

Completed designs can be displayed along with the stimulus materials. If the children make a large version of the design voted the best, this could be mounted centrally over the display.

Other aspects of the Geography PoS covered

1c; 2; 3f; 5a.

Reference to photocopiable sheet

Photocopiable page 151 is for the children to design a joint coat of arms which could be used if their locality and the contrasting overseas locality were to twin, as many towns and cities do.

It's twins!

Name _____ Date _____

Design a joint coat of arms for your two localities. Write their names in the spaces at the bottom.

Assessment

The activities in Chapters One to Five have suggestions for formative assessment included with them. Some of the photocopiable sheets relating to these activities are also suitable for summative assessment. These photocopiable sheets are marked with the ✍ icon.

This chapter contains supplementary assessment activities aimed specifically at a summative outcome. The activities have been designed to compliment the activities in the first five chapters of the book and they relate to photocopiable pages 152 to 157.

Each activity includes an explanation of its context and how it might best be introduced to the children, a note on how it relates to the Programme of Study and suggestions on the desired assessment outcome. Each one can be completed by children individually.

Much of geographical learning at Key Stage 2 is through the children's local area and therefore teaching needs to be tailored to that area. Summative assessment activities should be viewed in the light of wider geographical work the children have been involved in.

GEOGRAPHICAL VOCABULARY

Explanation
This is a cloze procedure in which the children select words from the bottom of the sheet to fit into each of the gaps in the text. The text includes important geographical words and uses the idea of providing an introduction to Earth for a visitor from Mars. Less fluent readers may need you to read the text to them before they start.

Reference to PoS
Geographical skills 3a.

Desired outcome
The children should be able to use clues in the text to help them place the missing words in the correct space. When analysing the children's responses check whether any inaccurate answers make any sense at all.

gibneohur

alurr

nocitnetni

isecit

natcised

SYMBOLS AND KEYS 1

Explanation
The children are asked to draw symbols for ten fairground activities in places of their choice on an empty map of a fairground. There is room for each activity to appear on the map once. The children have to design a key at the bottom of the sheet.

Reference to PoS
Geographical skills 3c.

Desired outcome
It is important that the children are left to design the key themselves. When analysing the work check that the children have used symbols as they were asked to and not just drawn the activities. When looking at the children's keys check that they have redrawn each of their symbols the same as on their map.

SYMBOLS AND KEYS 2

This assessment activity can be done by children who have been introduced to the symbols used by the Ordnance Survey. The symbols used on the 1:50 000 (Landranger) are recommended. The children should first decide which of the roads on the sheet is the motorway and which is the 'A' road, and colour them appropriately. The children design the rest of the map including one of each of the other listed features using its Ordnance Survey symbol. They then design a key using these symbols.

Reference to PoS
Geographical skills 3c.

Desired outcome
The children should complete the activity using the symbols as shown in the key of any Ordnance Survey 1:50 000 (Landranger) map sheet. Check that they have used the correct symbols and labelled them.

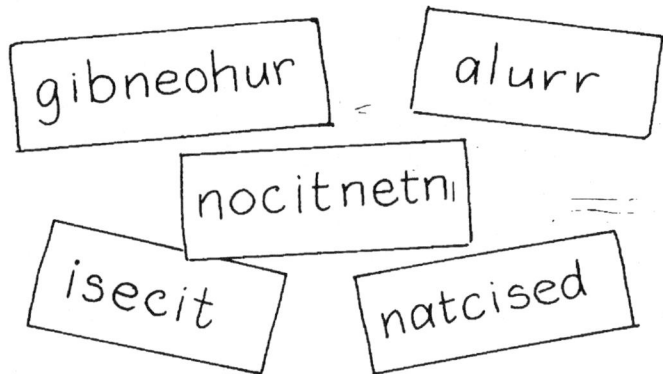

Suburban planner

Name _____ Date _____

▲ You have to plan a new area of suburb. The motorway and an 'A' road are already shown.

All the fun of the fair

Name _____ Date _____

This is a plan of a fairground. The entrance, paths and activity areas are shown.

Welcome to earth

Name _____ Date _____

You have come from the planet Mars which is our nearest _____. At first you landed in the countryside. This _____ area has which are very small and are called _____. Most people here earn a living through _____. Larger built up areas are called _____ and very large ones are called _____. Some of these are now joined together to make very large _____ areas.

The capital city of this _____ is London which is one of the largest in the _____ of Europe. The whole of this area is north of the _____ but the _____ runs through London.

To help you get around you will find it useful to use a _____. The scale on this will help you work out the _____ between places. If you need to know what _____ you are going in you could use a compass.

Our atmosphere has lots of different kinds of _____. You might get wet if there is heavy _____ and it might be too cold for you to measure the _____ with a _____.

While you are in the city travel round using our _____ system. You can buy food in a _____ area and enjoy yourself at a park, theatre or other _____ place. As you travel round you may see factories and other types of _____. You may come across churches, mosques and other places of _____. If you wish to make friends with any Earth people and find out about our homes, look for a _____ area.

Put these words in the correct gaps to help welcome the Martion to Earth.

leisure	continent	distance	cities	industry
settlements	worship	retail	rural	weather
country	thermometer	map	temperature	urban
agriculture	neighbour	direction	rainfall	equator
villages	prime meridian	transport	towns	residential

ISLAND CASTLE

Explanation

This activity involves the children in mapping at two different scales. They draw a map of an island and a map of a castle which is on that island. They then prove whether they can understand the concept of scale by adding a number to a scale line for each map, writing in the distance on the ground that 1cm on the map represents and then completing the ratio scales for the two maps. They also have to specify which map is at the larger scale and which one is at the smaller scale.

Reference to PoS

Geographical skills 3c.

Desired outcome

The children should draw a smaller scale map in the upper box and a larger scale map in the lower box and record this fact at the bottom of the sheet. Check that the information on scale is feasible. At the very least, the numbers given for the upper map should be higher than the numbers for the lower map. Reasonable numbers might be:

Upper map (island)	– scale line	= 500m
	– 1cm on the map	= 10 000cm
	– 1:	= 10 000
Lower map (castle)	– scale line	= 50m
	– 1cm on the map	= 1 000cm
	– 1:	= 1 000

SUPERMARKET PLAN

Explanation

Children use this activity to prove that they can work out the four-figure grid reference of features on a map and that they can use the grid to locate features when they have been given the four-figure grid reference.

It is important that children remember the conventions whereby you locate the space by looking at the numbers on the lines below and to the left and that you use eastings (the numbers along the bottom) before you use northings (the numbers up the left side).

Reference to PoS

Geographical skills 3d.

Desired outcome

The table should be completed with the following four-figure grid references:

0503, 0303, 0505, 0607, 0407, 0501, 0108, 0205.

The letters used in the 'new part of supermarket' key should be correctly located on the map.

Ships ahoy!

Name _____

Date _____

▲ Use the scale and compass direction rose to help you fill in the table.

BUSY SHIPS

Explanation
The children use the distance scale and compass direction rose to help them complete the table at the bottom of the sheet. To complete the sheet correctly the children will have to understand how to measure distance using a scale and how to measure direction of objects from a given point. It may help children to draw lines on the sheet between the dot indicating the mid-point of the 'Sea Lion' and the dots at the mid-points of the other ships. Children will have to understand that it is the direction *from* the 'Sea Lion' to the other ships which is being measured and not the other way round.

Reference to PoS
Geographical skills 3d.

Desired outcome
The table should be completed as follows:
The 'Sea Horse' is 10km north of the 'Sea Lion'.
The 'Walrus' is 8km east of the 'Sea Lion'.
The 'Porpoise' is 6km south-west of the 'Sea Lion'.
The 'Albatross' is 4km north-east of the 'Sea Lion'.
The 'Starfish' is 2km south-east of the 'Sea Lion'.
The 'Guppy' is 10km north-west of the 'Sea Lion'.
The 'Dolphin' is 6km south of the 'Sea Lion'.
The 'Kittiwake' is 5km west of the 'Sea Lion'.

MY ADDRESS

Explanation
This activity provides a check that children have a proper understanding of how their locality is set within a broader geographical context (a suburb is within a town is within a county and so on).

Give each child a piece of A4 paper and ask that they write their full address in the middle. For fun, encourage them to extend the information beyond the normal postal address as in the following example:

> Miss Patsy Cake
> 21 Fondant Street
> Great Kipling
> Bakewell
> Icingshire
> England
> United Kingdom
> Europe
> World

Tell the children to draw a line from each of the lines of the address to a space somewhere else on the sheet and to list other places which are also within each of these parts of the address (for example, for England the child might list several other English towns and cities; for Great Kipling the child might list other streets in the suburb/village).

Reference to PoS
1d; Places 4/5e.

Desired outcome
Children should end up with a sheet containing their own 'expanded' address which is then surrounded by lists containing other places which are similar in their type and scale to the ones in the main address.

GEOGRAPHY
KS2: PLACES

WHERE DO WE BUY THEM?

Explanation
We buy different types of goods and services from different places. We are prepared to travel different amounts of distance to buy things. The more we pay for items and the less frequently we buy them, the greater the distance we will travel.

We would happily travel to a neighbouring town or city to shop for a new bed or television, for example, but we would normally only travel a short distance to buy a newspaper or a bottle of milk. By studying these habits, children become more aware of the links which exist between their locality and other places.

Ask the children to think of a shopping list of six, eight, ten or more goods and/or services which they would buy from retailers of different sizes and which they would travel different distances to purchase. Get them to list these in order, according to how far they would travel for them (the shortest distance first). Using maps and other information, the children can then research and list the distances they would need to travel in order to buy the items they have chosen, and the names of the shops and their locations.

Reference to PoS
1d; Places 4/5e.

Desired outcome
Children should end up with a list of places from where their families buy goods and services. This list should be in order of distance travelled and should have the distance and the location of the shop listed next to each item/service.

A completed list might look something like this:

Newspaper	100m	corner shop
Potatoes	250m	local grocers
Weekly shopping	2km	supermarket
Pair of trousers	3km	high street shop
Television	7km	out of town shopping centre
Car	15km	neighbouring town

Involve the children in interpreting their list:
▲ Why is it that they might travel further for some items?
▲ How do they travel to each place?
▲ How much does it cost to travel to these places?
▲ How much does each item cost to buy?
▲ Is there any relation between these four factors?

OUR PLACE AND YOURS

Explanation
Each child writes a short (say half a side) piece about the contrasting UK locality being studied. Encourage the children to include as much descriptive detail as possible.

Once they have done this, ask them to underline those words which describe characteristics which are similar to their own local area in one colour and words which describe differences in another colour.

Reference to PoS
Places 4/5b.

Desired outcome
Each child should end up with a piece of descriptive writing which includes words underlined in two different colours. Check that the children have successfully differentiated between characteristics which are similar and different.

IN THE FUTURE

Explanation
An important concept in geography is that our world is constantly in a state of change. Some places change quickly while others seem to change very little. In their studies of a contrasting UK locality, children should address the issue of what is changing in this other locality, why these changes are happening and whether they think these changes are for the better.

Ask the children to draw a picture of how they think the locality might look in the future (say in 10 or 20 years' time).

This done, ask the children to annotate their picture labelling the major changes. Discuss the differences between 'human' and 'physical' features and help the children identify 'environmental issues'. Encourage them to identify how these features might change and develop in the future. (Did they show any of these in their picture?) The children could write explanations of the changes on a separate piece of paper.

Reference to PoS
Places 4/5d.

Desired outcome
Look for pictures which are feasible versions of the future for the locality you are studying. The children's annotations should include references to changes in the 'human' world, the 'physical' world and 'environmental issues'. Of these the hardest to think of may be changes in the 'physical' world.

ADVERTISING CAMPAIGN

Explanation
It is important that children recognise that there are similarities and differences between the contrasting overseas locality they are studying and their own home locality. Provide each child with two pieces of poster paper of the same size. Tell the children to research, if necessary, and list, in rough,

characteristics in the following categories indicating which are the same and those which are different in each locality:
▲ food;
▲ buildings;
▲ clothes;
▲ plants;
▲ animals;
▲ jobs;
▲ schools;
▲ transport.
An example for food might be:
▲ same – you can buy pizza here;
▲ different – people eat cheese for breakfast.

Ask the children to make two posters using drawn pictures based on the information in their lists. One poster should be to 'sell' the overseas locality to people who like the places they visit to be like home. The other should be to 'sell' it to people who like the places they visit to be different from home.

Reference to PoS
Places 4/5b.

Desired outcome
Two posters which each take the form of a montage of pictures. One is made up of drawn pictures depicting features of the contrasting overseas locality which are similar to the children's own local area and the other should depict features which are different from their own local area.

WHAT IS MISSING?

Explanation
Discuss with the children what physical and human features are typical of the overseas locality you are studying. Provide the children with a photograph of part of this locality.

The children stick the photograph in the middle of a larger piece of paper and then continue drawing around the central image, guessing what the surroundings might be like.

Reference to PoS
1b; Skills 3e; Places 4/5a.

Desired outcome
Children who have a good understanding of the physical and human features typical of the area they are studying will have included features relevant to the central photograph. If the area you are studying is on a plain in the middle of India, a child who has drawn a large mountain slope on one side of the picture will have missed the point. Children operating at a good level of understanding will have included physical and human features which are appropriate.

Photocopiables

The pages in this section can be photocopied for use in the classroom or school which has purchased this book, and do not need to be declared in any return in respect of any photocopying licence.

They comprise a varied selection of both pupil and teacher resources, including pupil worksheets, resource material and record sheets to be completed by the teacher or children. The photocopiable sheets are related to individual activities in the book; the name of the activity is indicated at the top of the sheet, together with a page reference indicating where the lesson plan for that activity can be found.

Individual pages are discussed in detail within each lesson plan, accompanied by ideas for adaptation where appropriate – of course, each sheet can be adapted to suit your own needs and those of your class. Sheets can also be coloured, laminated, mounted on to card, enlarged and so on where appropriate.

Many sheets have spaces provided for children's names and for noting the date on which each sheet was used. This means that, if so required, they can be included easily within any pupil assessment portfolio.

Photocopiable sheets 150 to 157 accompany the activities in the Assessment chapter; other sheets which can be used for summative assessment have been flagged with the ⬦ icon.

Describing places in our school (see page 14)

Our School

Name ______________________ Date ______________

leafy noisy boring muddy

concrete exposed calm grey natural green attractive

grass cold pretty quiet tarmac warm favourite

Our place:	
What is your place like? Write six describing words or phrases in these boxes.	Why? What reasons do you have for choosing these words?
1	
2	
3	
4	
5	
6	

sheltered busy ugly exciting

Using the right words (see page 15)

Link them up

Name _____   Date _____

▲ Draw a line to link each word with the picture it best describes.

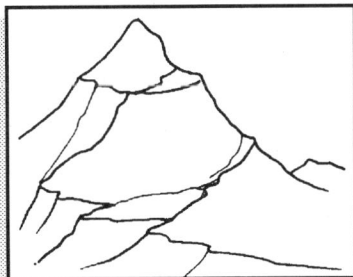

rural

hot

quiet

high

hilly

noisy

leafy

coastal

humid

urban

cold

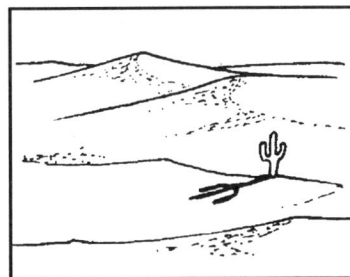

busy

low

flat

healthy

inland

polluted

enjoyable

**GEOGRAPHY
KS2: PLACES**

Measuring temperature (see page 17)

Hot and cold

Name _____   Date _____

Measuring the temperature around our school grounds

Places chosen as sample sites	Which places do you think will be the warmest and the coolest?	Results (temperature in °C)	The places with the warmest and the coolest temperatures

▲ Explain your findings...

What's in the picture? (see page 19)

Get the picture?

Name _____   Date _____

▲ Look carefully at this picture.
▲ Find as many clues as you can, then draw in the missing pieces.

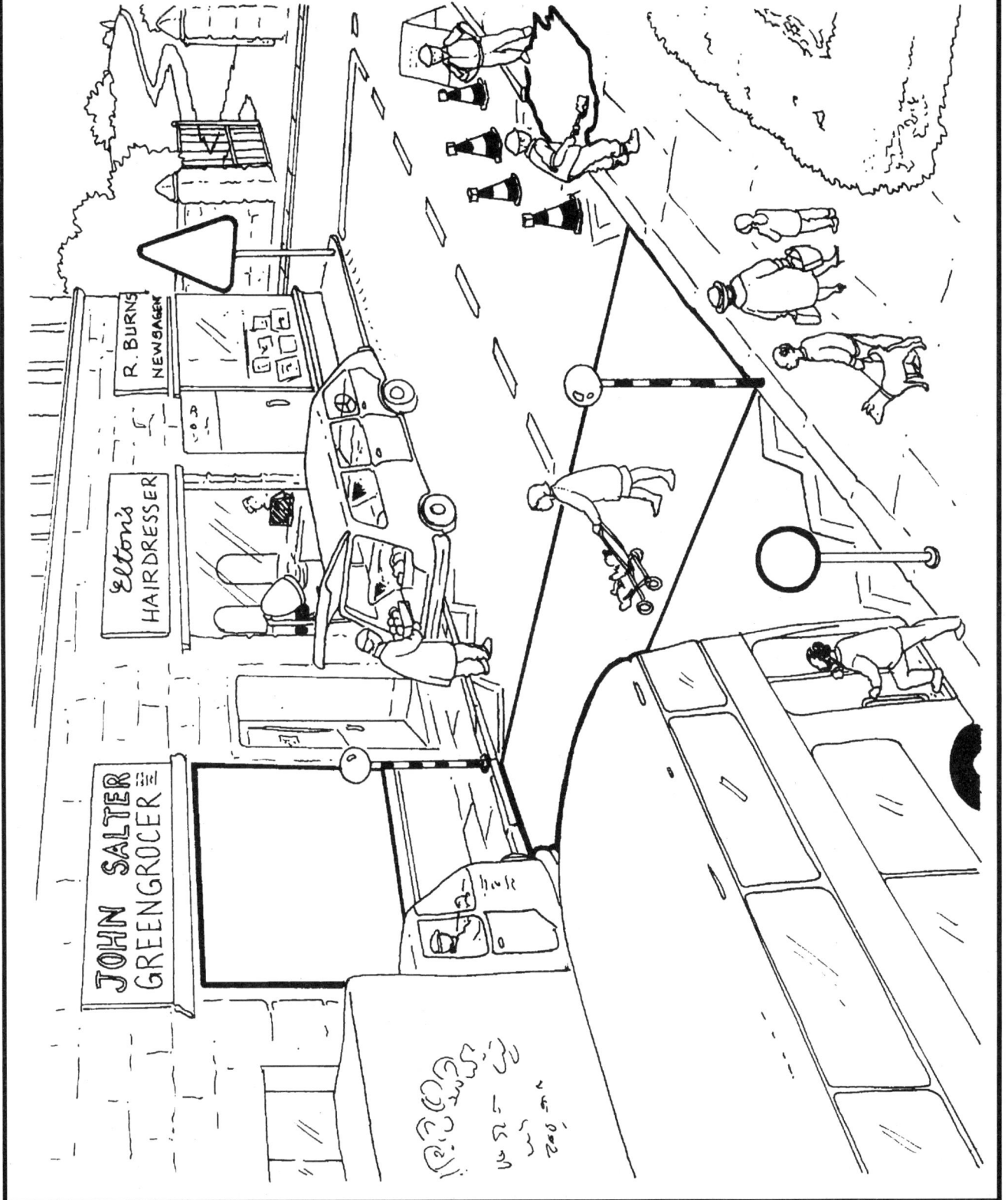

**GEOGRAPHY
KS2: PLACES**

Line graph – distances from home to school

Name _____   Date _____

▲ Write in the names of children in your class. Then draw a line graph to show the distances in kilometres from their homes to your school.

Line graph showing the distances in kilometres that children
in class .... live from .... school

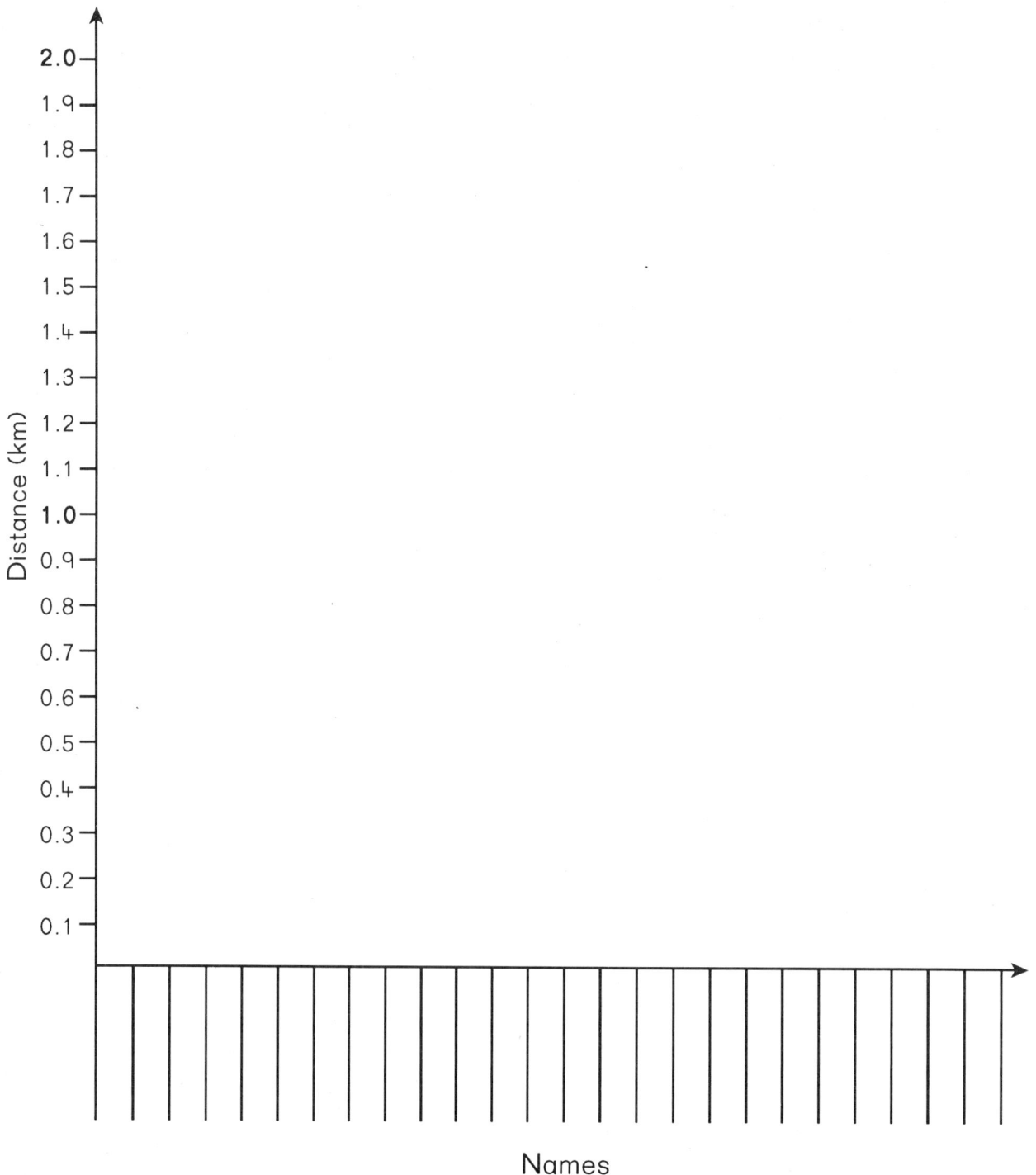

Distance (km)

2.0
1.9
1.8
1.7
1.6
1.5
1.4
1.3
1.2
1.1
1.0
0.9
0.8
0.7
0.6
0.5
0.4
0.3
0.2
0.1

Names

GEOGRAPHY
KS2: PLACES

Small, medium and large scale maps (see page 24)

Three maps

Name _____   Date _____

My table top
. . . .

Draw a close up view of your table top to fill this box. Add as much detail as you can. It is a **large scale** map. A large scale map shows more details.

> 1

My classroom
. . . .

Imagine that you are looking down at your classroom from the ceiling. Draw what you would see in this box. You are further away than when you drew your table so you can see more objects but not so many fine details. It will be a **medium scale** map.

> 2

My school
. . . .

Imagine that you were floating over the school in a hot air balloon. What would you see? Draw it here. This will be a **small scale** map. It covers a large area but does not show fine details.

> 3

Photocopiables

Different scale maps (see page 25)

Getting bigger!

Name _____   Date _____

Small scale map

_____
_____
_____
_____
_____

Medium scale map

Large scale map

_____
_____
_____
_____

▲ Copy these sentences beside the map square they belong to.

This square shows small details.   **This square shows a small area.**
This square shows a wide area.   **This square shows major landmarks.**

Curriculum Bank

GEOGRAPHY KS2: PLACES

Mapping the school (see page 27)

Scaling down

Name _____ Date _____

▲ Redraw this map of a school on to the grid below.
   Use one small square for each of the big squares.

Map of school

		Class 2	Class 3						
					Library	Class 4	Class 5	Class 6
		Hall							
Class 1							Class 7	
	Office							

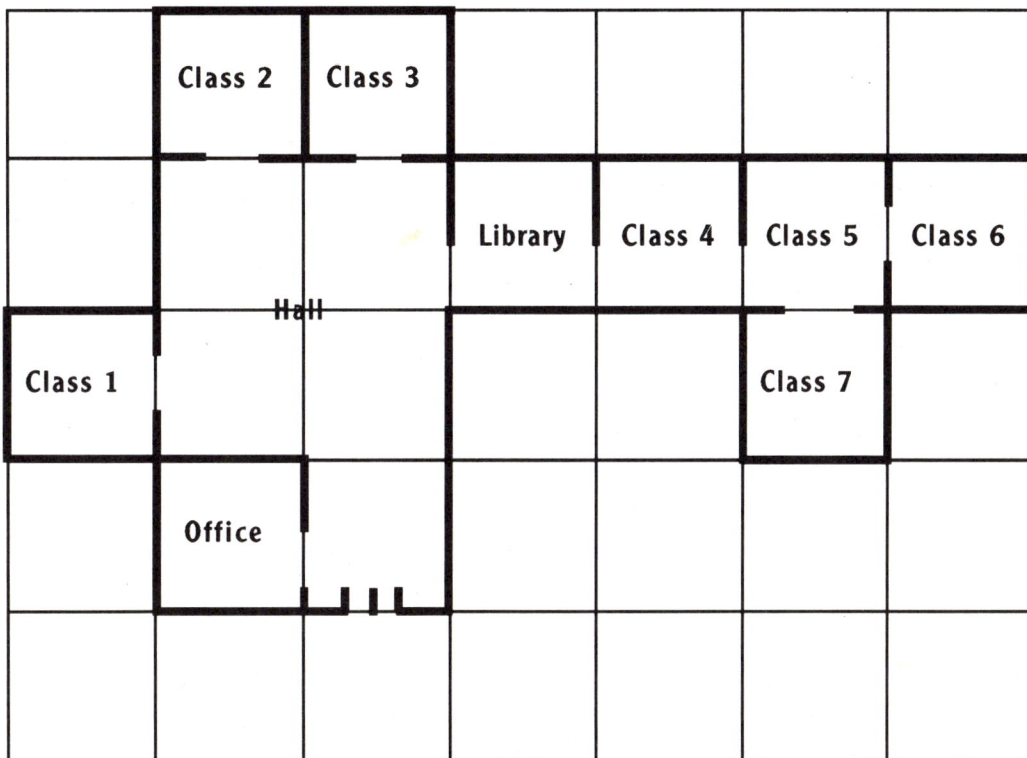

You should have enough room to design the school grounds around your new, smaller scale map of the school.

**GEOGRAPHY
KS2: PLACES**

Mapping the school (see page 27)

Scaling up

Name _____   Date _____

Map of school grounds

Road

Pond

School   Playground

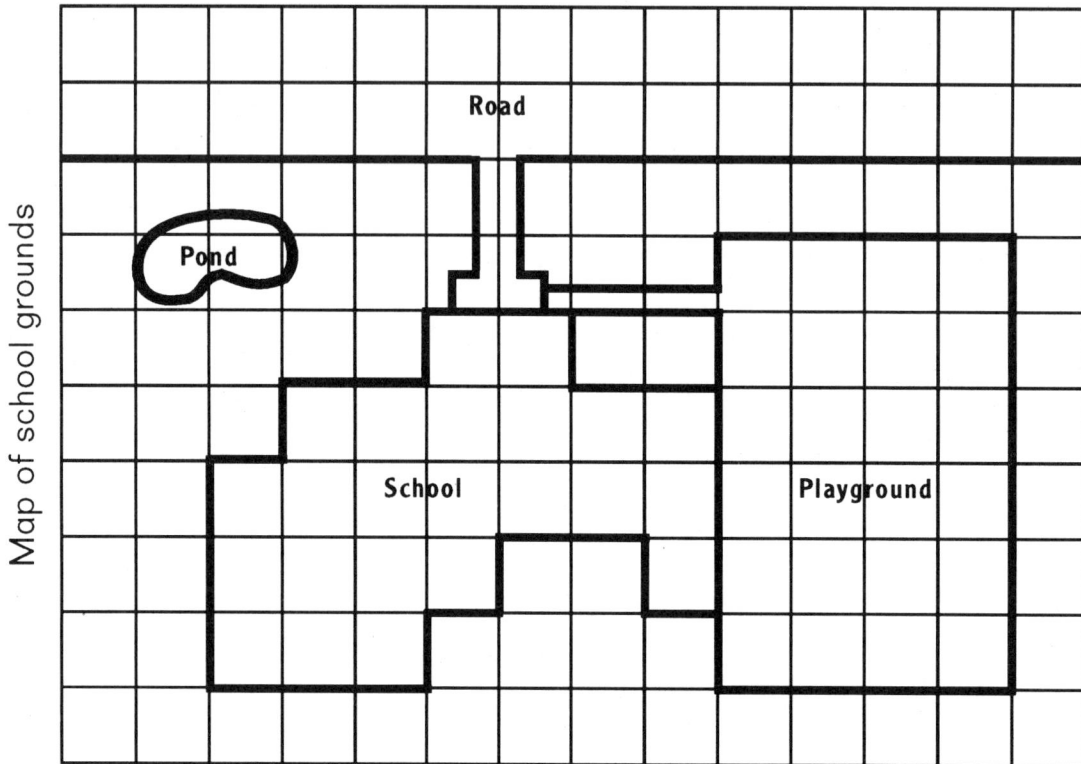

▲ Redraw a map of the school building only. Remember to show one small square in the map above as one large square in the map below.

Use your new, larger scale map to design the layout of the inside of the building.

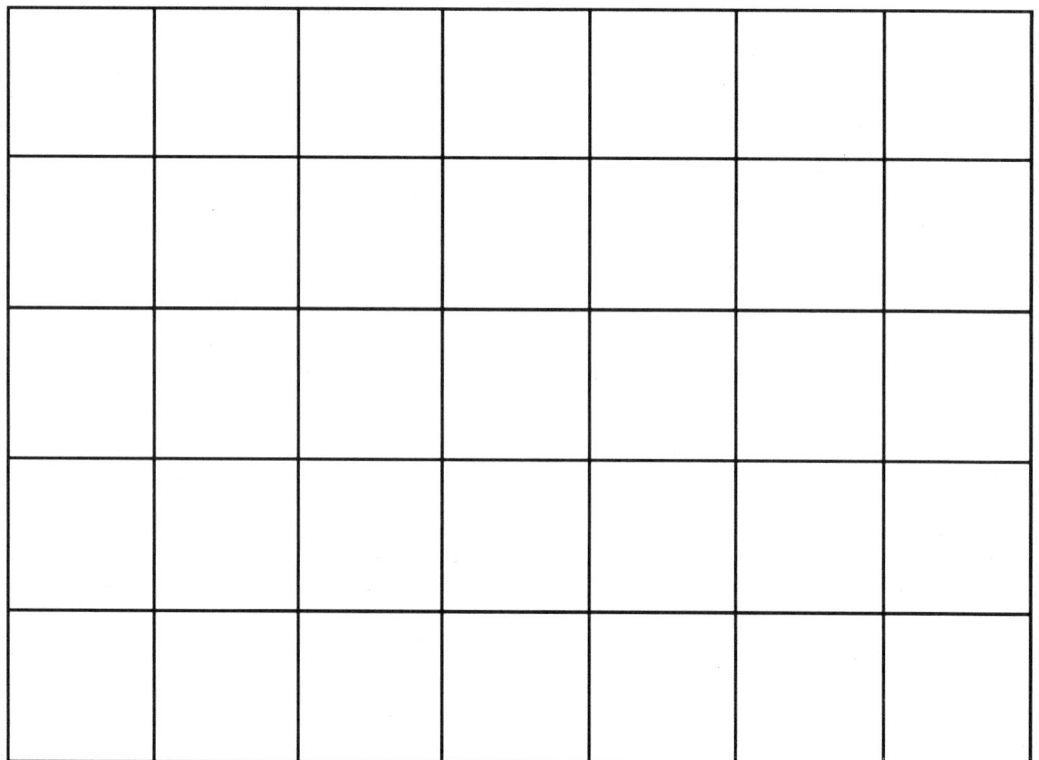

**GEOGRAPHY
KS2: PLACES**

Symbols and keys (see page 28)

Symbols in our area

Name _____   Date _____

Symbols around our school	Where we found it	What it means
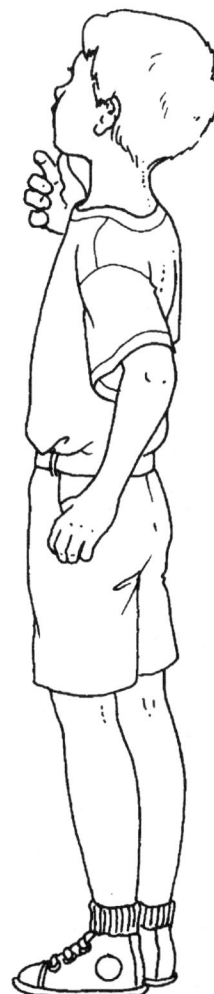	Road sign at side of road.	Warning! School ahead.

▲ Draw signs and symbols found near your school. Choose different types of signs and symbols. Write down where you found the signs and what they mean.

© Crown copyright

GEOGRAPHY KS2: PLACES

More symbols

Name _____ Date _____

▲ Fill in the blanks.
▲ Carefully design symbols to match the meanings.
▲ Write down meanings for the symbols printed here.

Symbol	What it means
⚡	
	Entrance for wheelchair users
☁	
🚫🚗	
	Walk on the left-hand side only
	Beware of dragons

Measuring distance (see page 37)

How far is it?

Name _____ Date _____

Points measured between	How far is it in a straight line?	How far is it using routeways?

TOWN 2 MILES

SMITH REMOVALS

TOWN 4 MILES

J. TROUT FISHMONGER

TOWN 6 MILES

**GEOGRAPHY
KS2: PLACES**

Photocopiables

Follow me!

Name _____   Date _____

Welcome to
Green Street School
School Tour Map

START
HERE

Street

Green

Head

Staff room

STAFF ROOM
Visitors
welcome
Please
knock

Entrance

Class 1

Toilets

Class 2

Class 3

Library

Dinner area

Hall

Class 4

Playground

Car Park

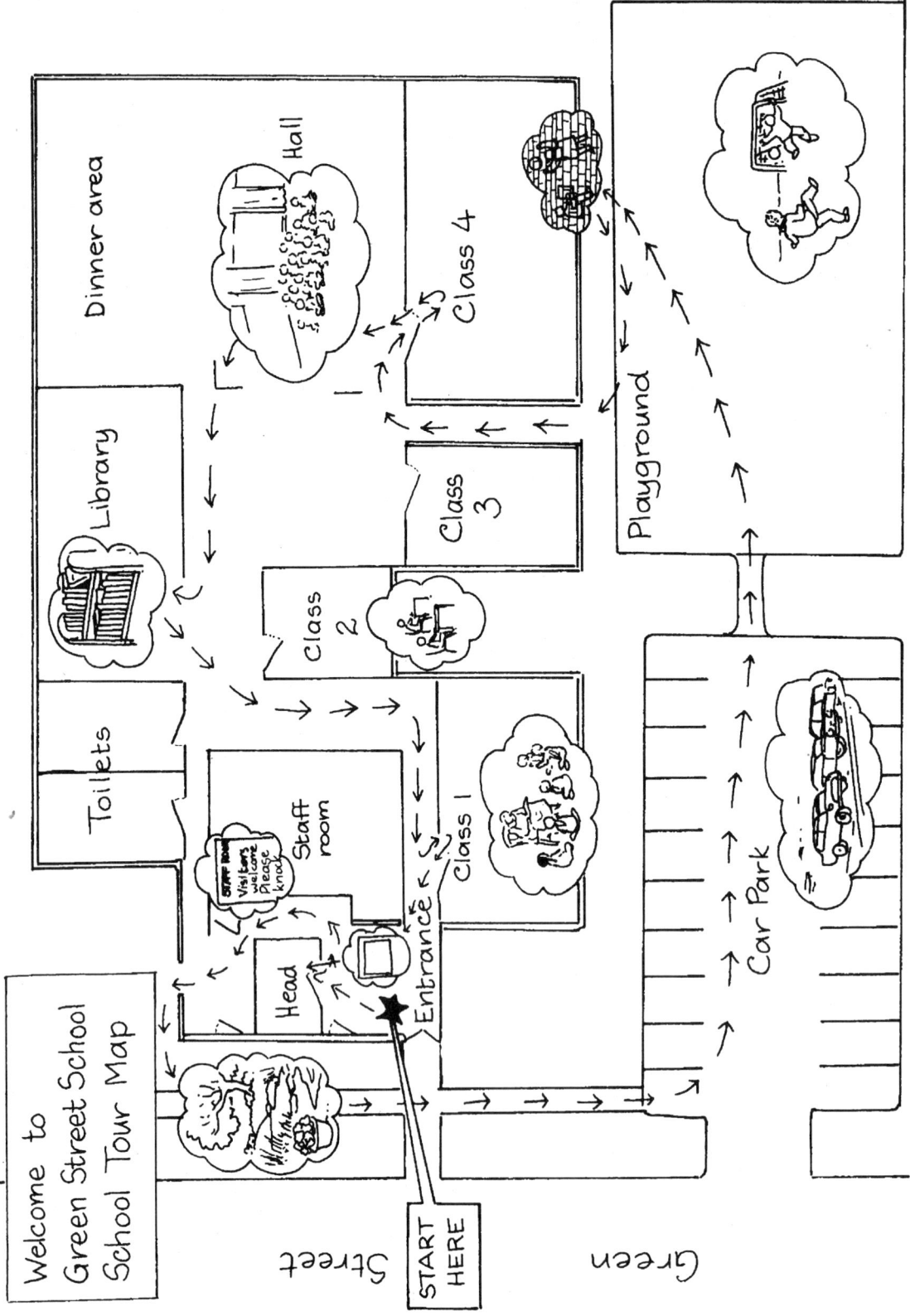

▲ Look at the route on this map. It is used to show visitors as much of Green Street School as possible. Imagine that you are a pupil at the school. Write a brief guide for visitors who follow the route.

Know your country (see page 42)

Traveller's tales

Name _____ Date _____

When in history?

Luggage?

How did you travel?

Main character: name and description	Other characters: names and descriptions

How long a journey?

Equipment?

Who did you meet?

▲ Order of places visited – include all the places in the boxes on photocopiable page 121.

Name of place	Description of place	What happened there
Starting place...		
Finishing place...		

GEOGRAPHY
KS2: PLACES

Welcome to Europe! (see page 44)

Come and meet Europe

Name _____   Date _____

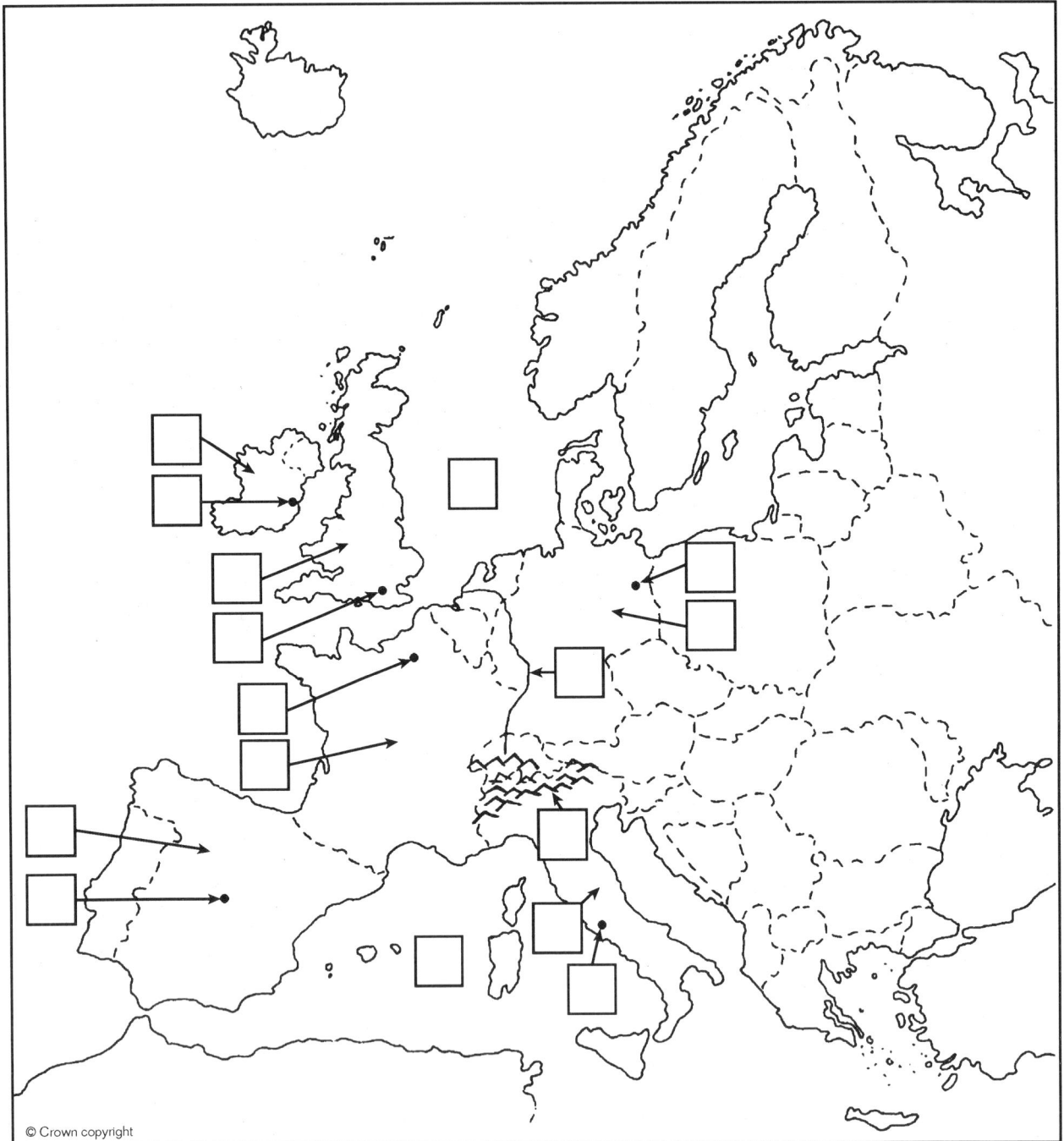

© Crown copyright

▲ Put these numbers in the correct boxes on the map.

1. The Alps	5. Germany	9. Madrid	13. River Rhine
2. Berlin	6. Ireland	10. Mediterranean Sea	14. Rome
3. Dublin	7. Italy	11. North Sea	15. Spain
4. France	8. London	12. Paris	16. United Kingdom

**GEOGRAPHY
KS2: PLACES**

Where in the world? (see page 47)

Where on earth is it?

Name _____   Date _____

▲ Write the numbers in the correct places on the map.

Continents	
Europe	1
North America	2
South America	3
Africa	4
Oceania	5
Antarctica	6
Asia	7

Countries	
Canada	11
USA	12
Brazil	13
Russian Federation	14
China	15
India	16
Indonesia	17
Australia	18

Mountains	
Himalayas	8
Rockies	9
Andes	10

Canals	
Suez Canal	19
Panama Canal	20

Cities	
New York	21
Buenos Aires	22
Paris	23
Cairo	24
Bombay	25
Sydney	26

Poles	
North Pole	27
South Pole	28

Tropics	
Tropic of Capricorn	29
Tropic of Cancer	30

Oceans	
Atlantic Ocean	31
Pacific Ocean	32
Arctic Ocean	33
Indian Ocean	34

Deserts	
Sahara Desert	35

Rivers	
River Mississippi	36
River Amazon	37
River Nile	38

Imaginary lines	
Equator	39
Prime Meridian	40

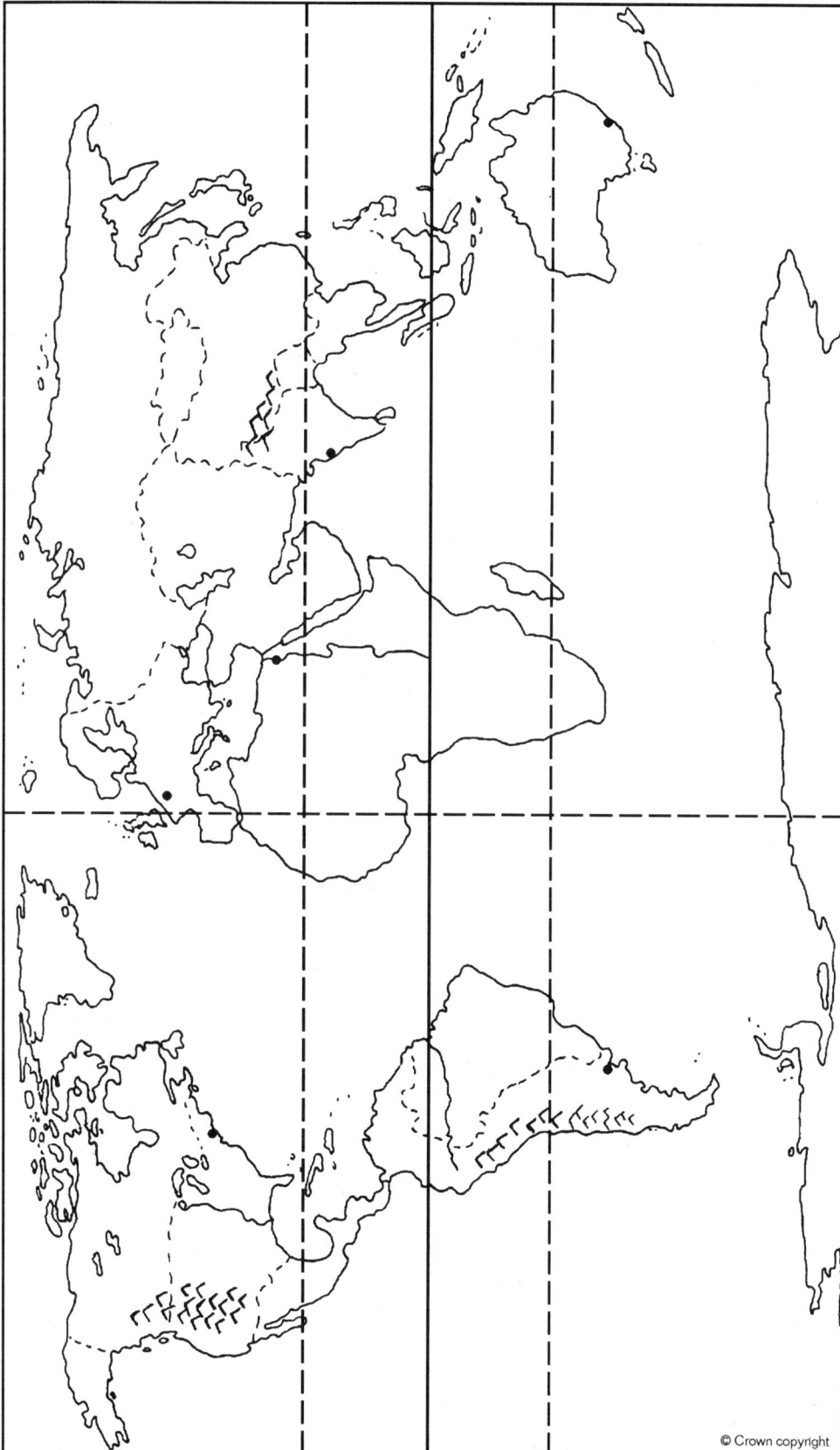

© Crown copyright

GEOGRAPHY
KS2: PLACES

Your locality (see page 50)

Your Place

Name _____ Date _____

▲ Colour in the places which are in your school's local area.

▲ Think about your local area. Draw a picture of each of these places.

The quietest place   The busiest road
The largest building   The smallest building

▲ Label each one to say where it is.
▲ Write a description of each of the places saying as much about them as you can.

Physical features (see page 52)

If there were no buildings...

Name _____   Date _____

▲ Draw what your locality looks like now...

When you draw your locality, imagine you are looking down on to it from the side.

▲ Draw what your locality would have looked like before people had ever changed it.

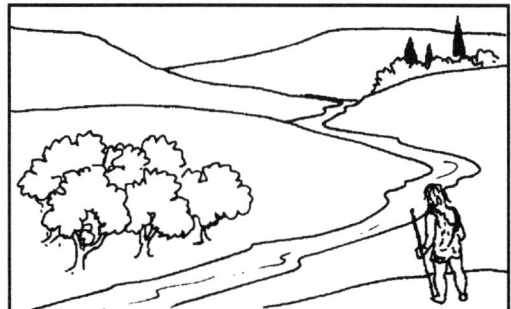

Human features (see page 53)

Guidebook

Name _____   Date _____

A guidebook to

_____

Homes

Transport

Leisure

Shops

Work

Our school

**GEOGRAPHY
KS2: PLACES**

Your locality's environment (see page 55)

Getting to school

Name _____   Date _____

Children in my class	Methods for getting to school						Preferred methods for getting to school					
	Walking	Bicycle	Taxi	Car	Bus	Other	Walking	Bicycle	Taxi	Car	Bus	Other
Tally												
Number												

**GEOGRAPHY
KS2: PLACES**

Your locality's environment (see page 55)

Travel bar graphs

Name _____   Date _____

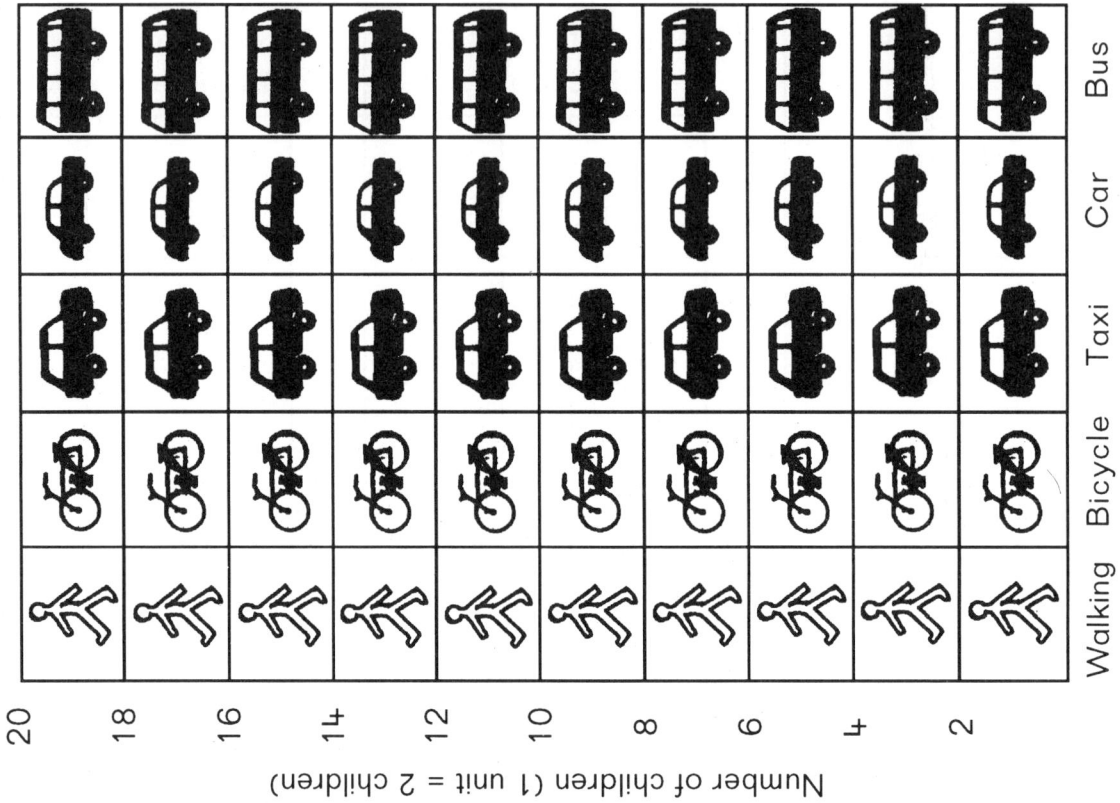

How children in our class would like to get to school

Number of children (1 unit = 2 children)

Walking Bicycle Taxi Car Bus

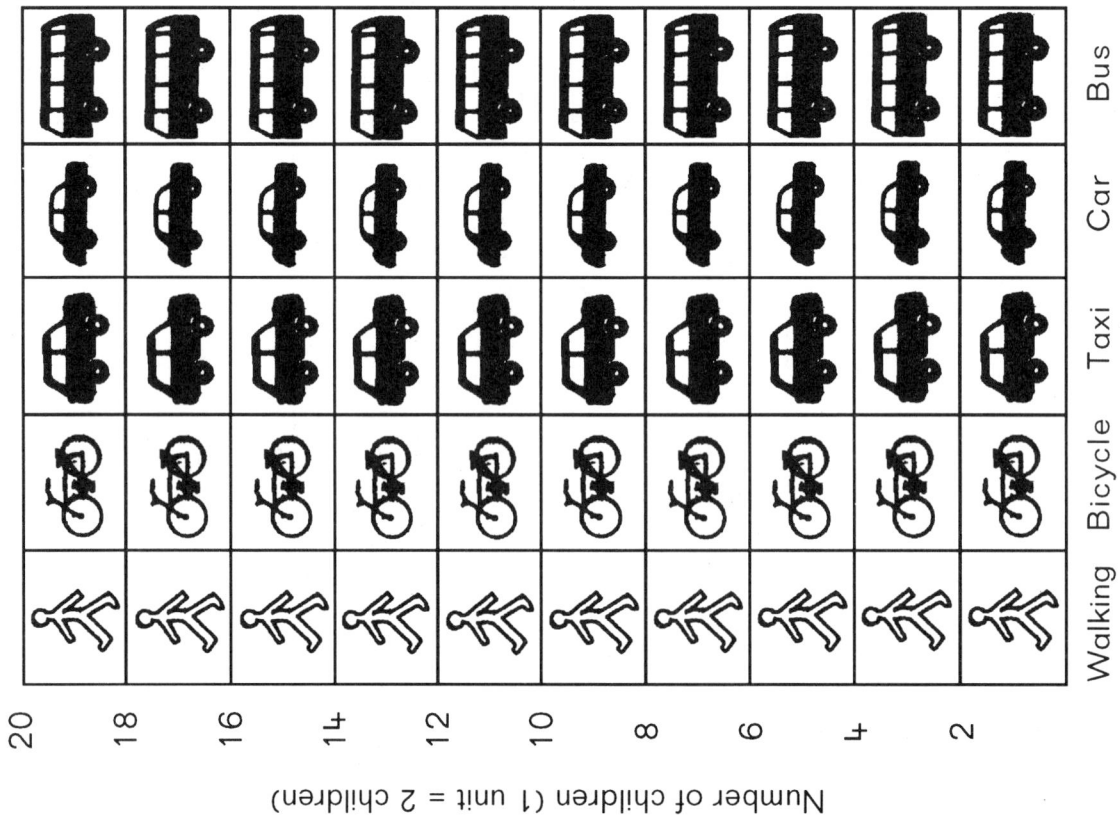

How children in our class get to school

Number of children (1 unit = 2 children)

Walking Bicycle Taxi Car Bus

▲ Using the charts on page 127, colour in the right number of units on the 'Number of children' axis.

**GEOGRAPHY
KS2: PLACES**

Photocopiables

Human activity in your locality (see page 57)

Buildings people in our area use

Name _____   Date _____

A map of the local area around our school

Key
⌐L Roads
Bus route
S Bus stop

Homes	Employers	Busy leisure
Shops that are used often	Education	Quiet leisure
Shops that are not used often	Medical	Worship

▲ Write an explanation of the bus route you have chosen on a separate sheet of paper.

Curriculum Bank

129

Change in your locality (see page 58)

Change checklist

Name _____   Date _____

The Issue:

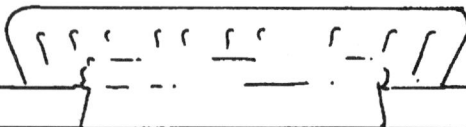

WHAT? ?	What is the change?
WHEN?	Is the change in the past/present/future?
WHERE?	Where in the locality is this change?
WHO?	Who can tell me more about the change? Who will have opinions about the change?
HOW?	How is the change going to take place?
WHY? ?	What are the reasons for this change?

▲ Use the answers to these questions to help you write your newspaper article.

**GEOGRAPHY
KS2: PLACES**

Links with where you live (see page 60)

Links with other places

Name _____   Date _____

	Footpaths	Bridleways	Tracks	Roads	A-roads	Motorways	Tramways	Railways	Canals	Rivers	Roundabouts	Car parks	Stations (bus)	Stations (rail)	Port	Airport	Names of places linked to where I live
National																	
Regional																	
Local																	

▲ Put ticks in the columns for the number of features identified on each of your maps.
▲ Write the names of places linking with your locality in the last column.

The same but different (see page 62)

A great place

Name _____   Date _____

The delights of

The place where
many people work

Where the children
go to school

One of the
best views

A typical home

A good place to enjoy yourself

**GEOGRAPHY
KS2: PLACES**

UK locality – Physical features (see page 67)

A place in the UK – the shape of the land

Name _____ Date _____

▲ Look carefully at the picture. Copy the same view *but* only include the physical features (those features which would be there even if no human had ever been to this place). Label your picture choosing from the list below.

river
volcano
shape
mountain
channel
glacier
valley
stream
river bank
plain
hill
mountain range
cliff
source
ocean
island
waterfall

GEOGRAPHY
KS2: PLACES

UK locality – human features (see page 69)

A day in the life of ...

This diary belongs to:

....

Address ....

....

....

Day ....

Month ....

Year ....

A picture of me...

My day at work

....

....

....

....

....

....

....

....

Where I work...

My job

....

....

....

Things I need for my job...

▲ Fill in this diary page as though you are a person who works in the locality you are studying. You must mention the names of real places, streets and places of work to make it realistic.

GEOGRAPHY
KS2: PLACES

Environmental issues 'radio' (see page 71)

Radio 'environment' Programme planning sheet 1

The radio show all about the environment

Date

Names of reporters/researchers

Where in the UK is the programme about?

Description of the area.

What is the environmental issue?

The main views people have on the issue.

Interviews.

How the issue might change the area.

Summary.

**GEOGRAPHY
KS2: PLACES**

Photocopiables

Environmental issues 'radio' (see page 71)

Radio 'environment' Programme planning sheet

Date

Names of reporters/researchers

Sally, Ahmed, Mark, Gemma

The radio show all about the environment

Where in the UK is the programme about?

Folkestone

Description of the area.

Small, old town. Chalky cliffs. Lots of fields. Near to port of Dover.

What is the environmental issue?

Channel tunnel comes out here. Has caused lots of disagreement among locals. Loss of green land. More traffic.

The main views people have on the issue.

Some angry at farmland being eaten up. Some don't like extra traffffic. Some pleased about it. Some think it will make their area richer. Workers pleased about new jobs in the area.

Interviews.

Tunnel manager – I am pleased that my company has brought so much new money to this area and has given so many local people new jobs. This tunnel is very important for all of Britain.
Local farmer – The company gave me a lot of money for my land, but to be honest I'm rather sad that I haven't got a farm any more.
Local villager – I think the new terminal is an eye-sore. It has really spoilt this area.

How the issue might change the area.

More traffic. New big roads. New railway. Less countryside. Some new jobs.

Summary.

Countryside used up. New jobs. More traffic and new roads. Important for Britain.

Curriculum Bank

138

People and localities in the UK (see page 73)

Features

Name _____   Date _____

Location being studied ....

Human features found	Physical features which had an effect on where things are	Existing human factors which had an effect on where things are
Housing estate	High place	Housing estate
Shopping centre/retail park	Low place	Shopping centre/retail park
Warehouse/factory	Flat place	Warehouse/factory
Main Road/motorway	Steep slope	Main Road/motorway
Railway line/sidings	Narrow valley	Railway line/sidings
Canal	Hill	Canal
Golf course/park	Slope facing a certain direction	Golf course/park
Swimming pool	Place with good views	Swimming pool
School/college	Wide river	School/college
Doctors/hospital	Narrow part of a river	Doctors/hospital
Industrial are/estate	Place with fertile soil	Industrial area/estate
Bridge/ferry	Place with poor soil	Bridge/ferry
Farm	Place with a gentle coastline	Farm
Football/sports ground	Place with a steep coastline	Football/sports ground
Bus station	Place exposed to the weather	Bus station
Railway station	Place sheltered from the weather	Railway station
Port area	Place with a lake	Port area
Tourism location	Rocky place	Tourism location
Waste disposal site	Forested place	Waste disposal site

▲ Ring human features shown on the map of your location in the first column. Draw arrows linking each of these features to any physical and existing human features which you think affected where the features in the first column were built.

Photocopiables

Changes in a UK locality (see page 74)

Past, Present and Future

Name _____   Date _____

Maryford in 1901

– The church had lots of land around it.
– Large trees stood in the graveyard.
– The old cottages were built.
– People rode in pony and traps.

The Past

Maryford nowadays

– A church hall has been built.
– Stone street has been built.
– The factory has been built.
– The graveyard is small but full.
– Lots of parked cars.

The locality now

Maryford in 2050

– The church has been re-built.
– The old cottages have been preserved.
– New parks have been created.
– Trams have replaced most cars.

The future

SHOPPERS WOR

Putting it on the map (see page 76)

Connect them up

Name _____   Date _____

Key:
- ◉ Capital
- ● City/Town
- ○ Village
- ≡ Motorway
- ⊦⊦⊦ Railway
- ⊨⊨ Railway station
- — Road
- ⛴ Port
- ✈ Airport
- ...... County/Region boundary

© Crown copyright

**GEOGRAPHY
KS2: PLACES**

This locality – that locality (see page 77)

What's the difference?

Name _____   Date _____

Contrasting UK locality

My school's locality

Key:

blue   Residential

red   Shopping

brown   Industrial/Commercial

green   Agricultural

pink   Leisure facilities

yellow   Educational

orange   Medical

purple   Places of worship (land/buildings)

grey   Transport/Communication

white   Other

▲ Transfer the coloured information from your two maps to these two grids.

GEOGRAPHY
KS2: PLACES

This locality – that locality (see page 77)

Are they the same?

Name _____

	My locality	Contrasting locality
Percentage of land used for different purposes in .... and		
Residential		
Shopping		
Industrial/Commercial		
Agricultural		
Leisure		
Educational		
Medical		
Worship		
Transport/Communication		
Other		

My locality

Percentage of Land/Buildings

100
90
80
70
60
50
40
30
20
10

Residential
Shopping
Industrial/Commercial
Agricultural
Leisure
Educational
Medical
Worship
Transport/Communication
Others

Contrasting UK Locality

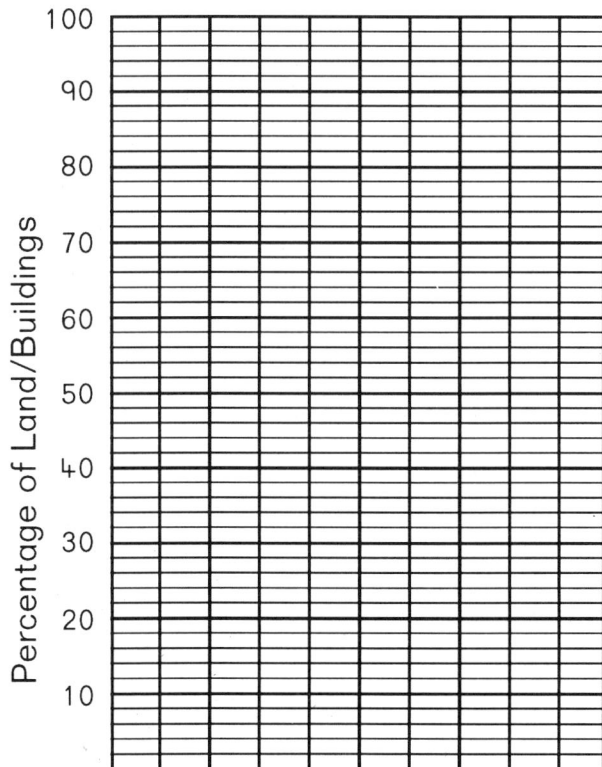

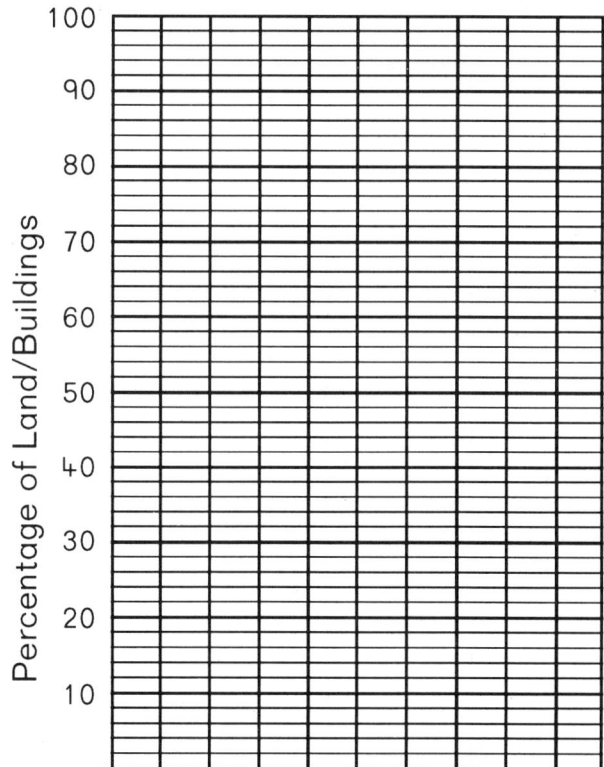

Percentage of Land/Buildings

100
90
80
70
60
50
40
30
20
10

Residential
Shopping
Industrial/Commercial
Agricultural
Leisure
Educational
Medical
Worship
Transport/Communication
Others

Photocopiables

Themes 1

Name _____ Date _____

Place being studied ....

Rivers, Streams, Lakes and Sea	Where found answer
Name of any ponds/lakes	
Name of any streams/rivers	
Name of any sea	
Where is the source of nearest river?	
Where is mouth of nearest river?	
Length of nearest river	
Weather and its effects	**Where found answer**
Three places people go to enjoy themselves if it rains	
Three places people go to enjoy themselves in good weather	

Photocopiables

Thematic studies and our UK locality (see page 79)

Themes 2

Name _____ Date _____

Place being studied ....

Homes, Buildings and Transport	Where found answer
Main building material	
How many people live in this place?	
How old is the oldest part of this place?	
What are the main ways of moving around this place?	
Quality of the environment	**Where found answer**
What is best about this place's environment?	
What is worst about this place's environment?	
What is changing about this place's environment?	

GEOGRAPHY
KS2: PLACES

All around the world (see page 82)

My quarter of the world

Name _____   Date _____

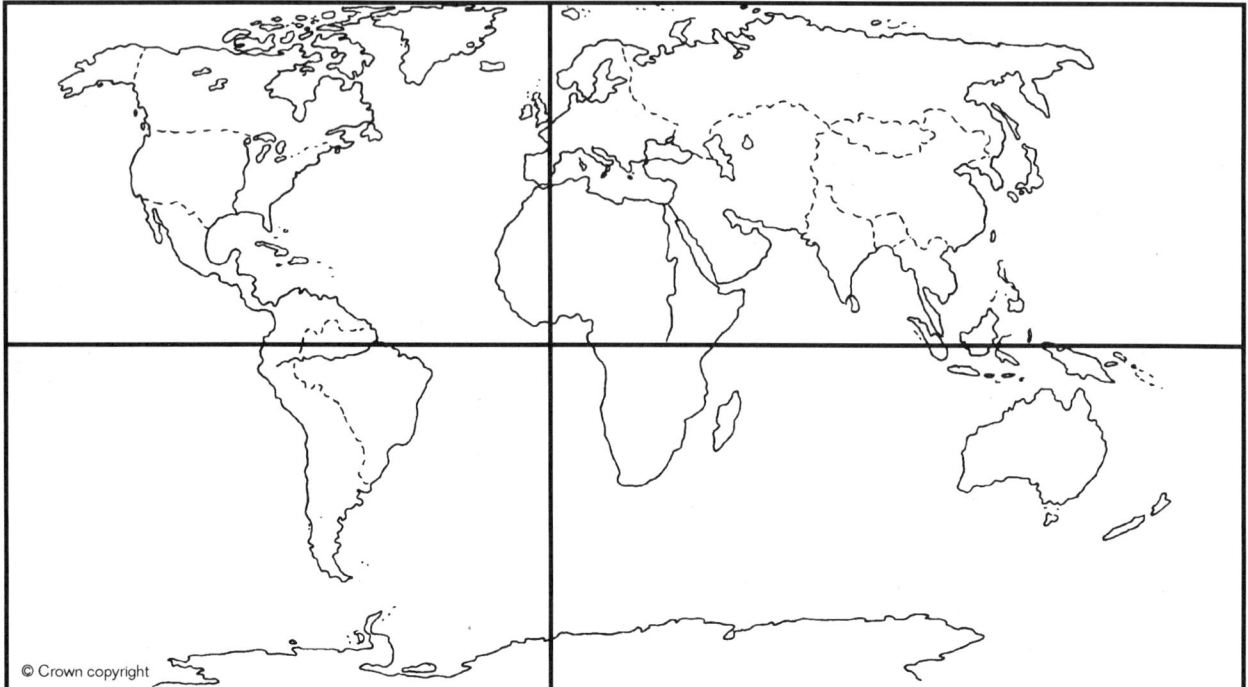

© Crown copyright

name of place	
continent and country	
city/town/village	
coastal/inland	
climate	
landscape	
language(s)	
ways of making a living	
name of place	
continent and country	
city/town/village	
coastal/inland	
climate	
landscape	
language(s)	
ways of making a living	

**GEOGRAPHY
KS2: PLACES**

Photocopiables

Colour it in

Name _____   Date _____

Colour
mountains (brown)
deserts (yellow)
rainforest (green)
sea/river (blue)

1 Rocky Mountains   5 South American   8 Australian Desert 13 Atlantic Ocean
2 Andes Mountains   Rainforest   9 River Rhine   14 Pacific Ocean
3 Ural Mountains   6 Central African 10 River Amazon   15 Indian Ocean
4 Himalayan   Rainforest   11 River Mississippi 16 Arctic Ocean
   Mountains   7 Sahara Desert   12 River Nile

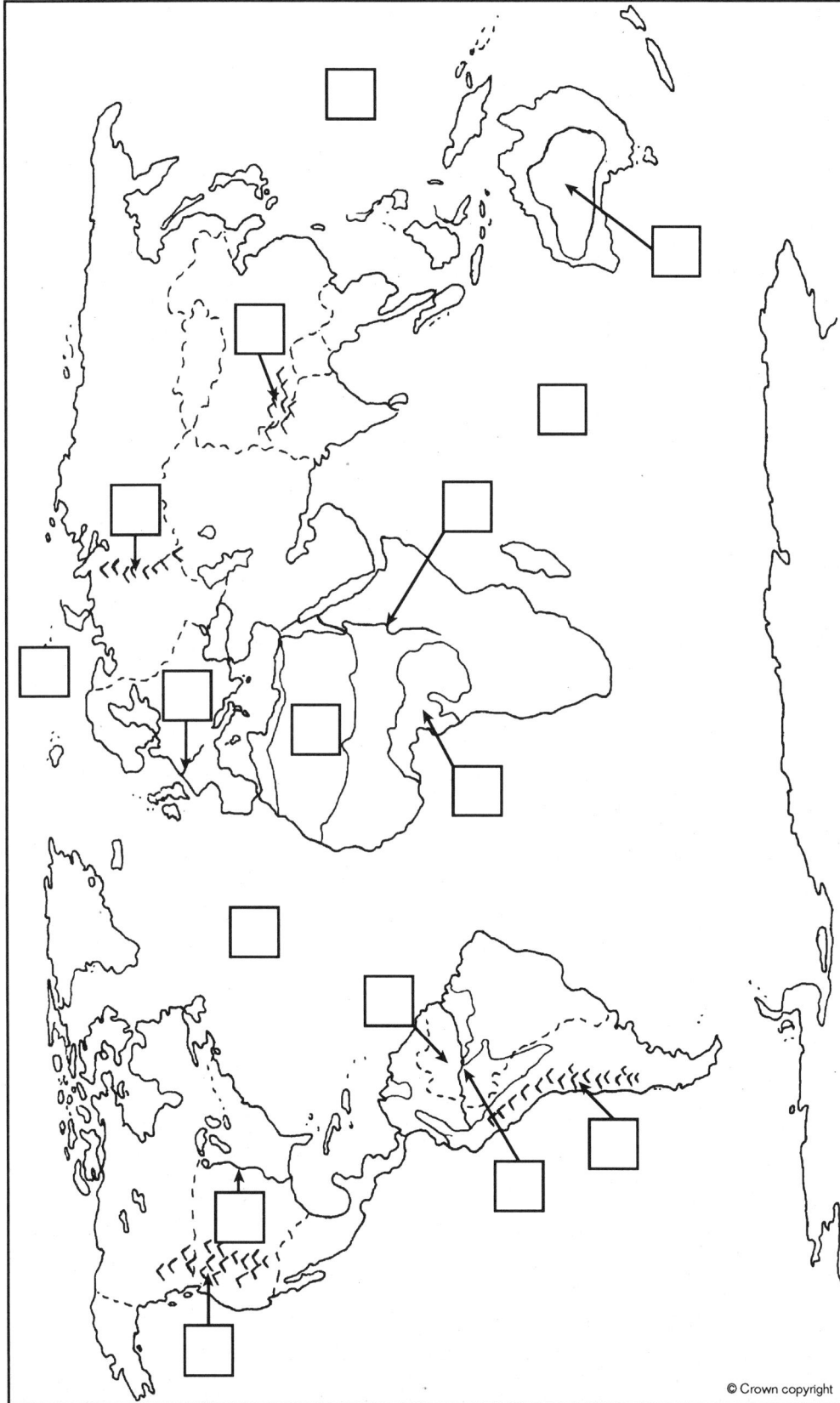

© Crown copyright

GEOGRAPHY
KS2: PLACES

Settlement skylines (see page 85)

Skylines

**GEOGRAPHY
KS2: PLACES**

Photocopiables

Environmental debate (see page 87)

The Indian Road

Name _____   Date _____

Indian Government:
'We are officials from the Indian Government. We are very keen that communications should be improved in our country so that people and materials can move around more easily. We will do our best to help those who are affected by the new road.'

Tea plantation official:
'My company must have up-to-date roads for our lorries to get the tea we grow to the port for export to other countries. Our company makes a lot of money from growing tea and employs a lot of local people. The land the road will be built on is less important than our plantation land.'

Village elder:
'My village will have to be knocked down for the new road. They say that they will build a new village for us, but we like our old one. We have been told we could earn money helping to build the new road – but what happens when it is finished?'

Local Indian farmer:
'This new road will use up most of my farmland. The government say they will give me some money but I don't know how much. I am worried that I will not find work on other people's farms. I had always wanted my children to take over my farm and to look after my wife and me when we are old.'

▲ Write arguments supporting each of the four groups of people on a separate sheet of paper and highlight the main differences of opinion.

Connections (see page 90)

Plane, Train, Ship, Car?

Name _____   Date _____

Cities on map: Tokyo, Beijing, New Delhi, Sydney, Wellington, Moscow, Nairobi, Pretoria, Cairo, Rome, London, New York, Ottawa, Caracas, Buenos Aires

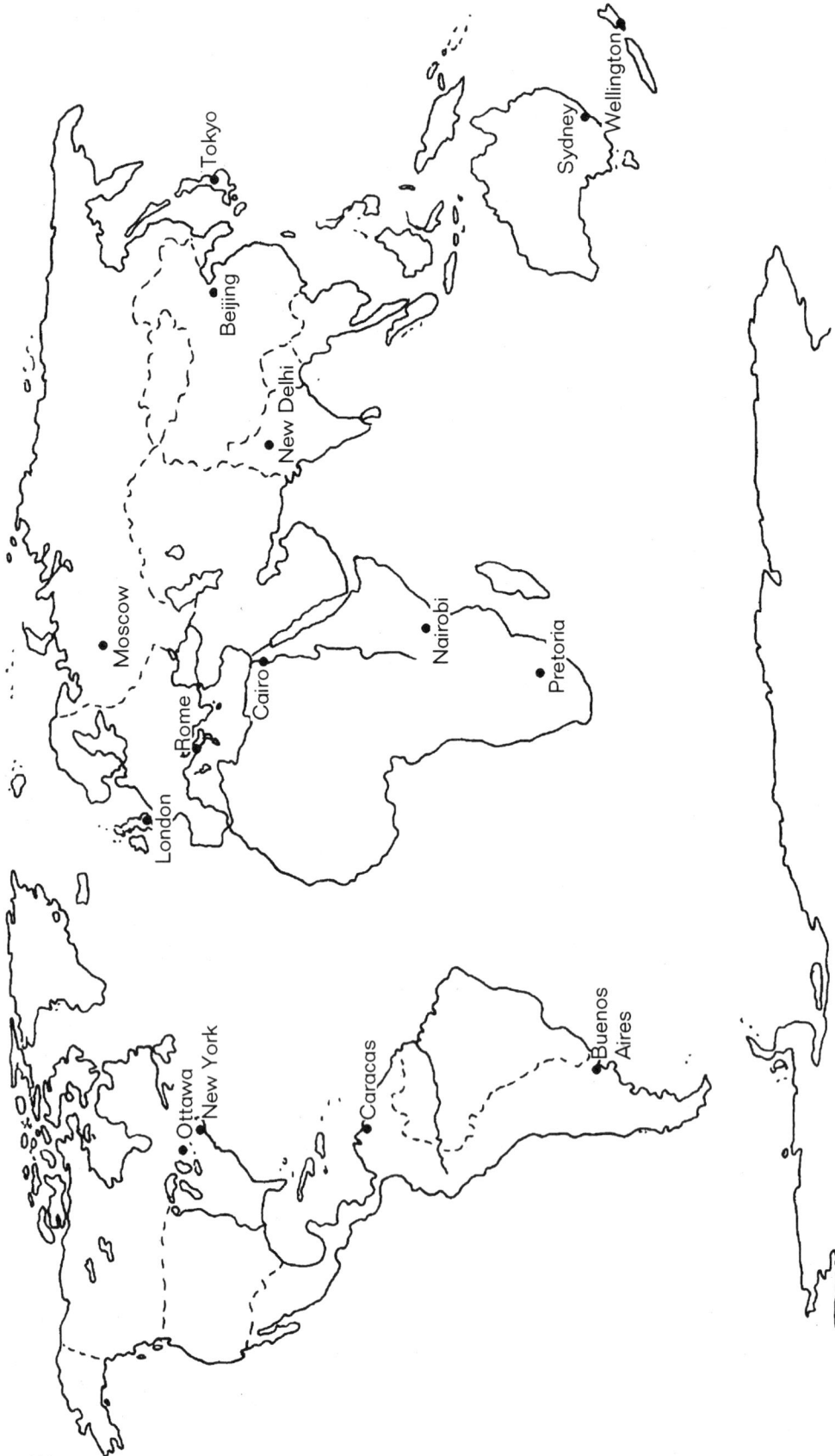

▲ Mark the place you are studying on this map of the world. Choose three of the cities shown on this map (including London). Mark routes between the place you are studying and each of the three cities.
▲ Design a key.

© Crown copyright

Twins (see page 91)

It's twins!

Name _____   Date _____

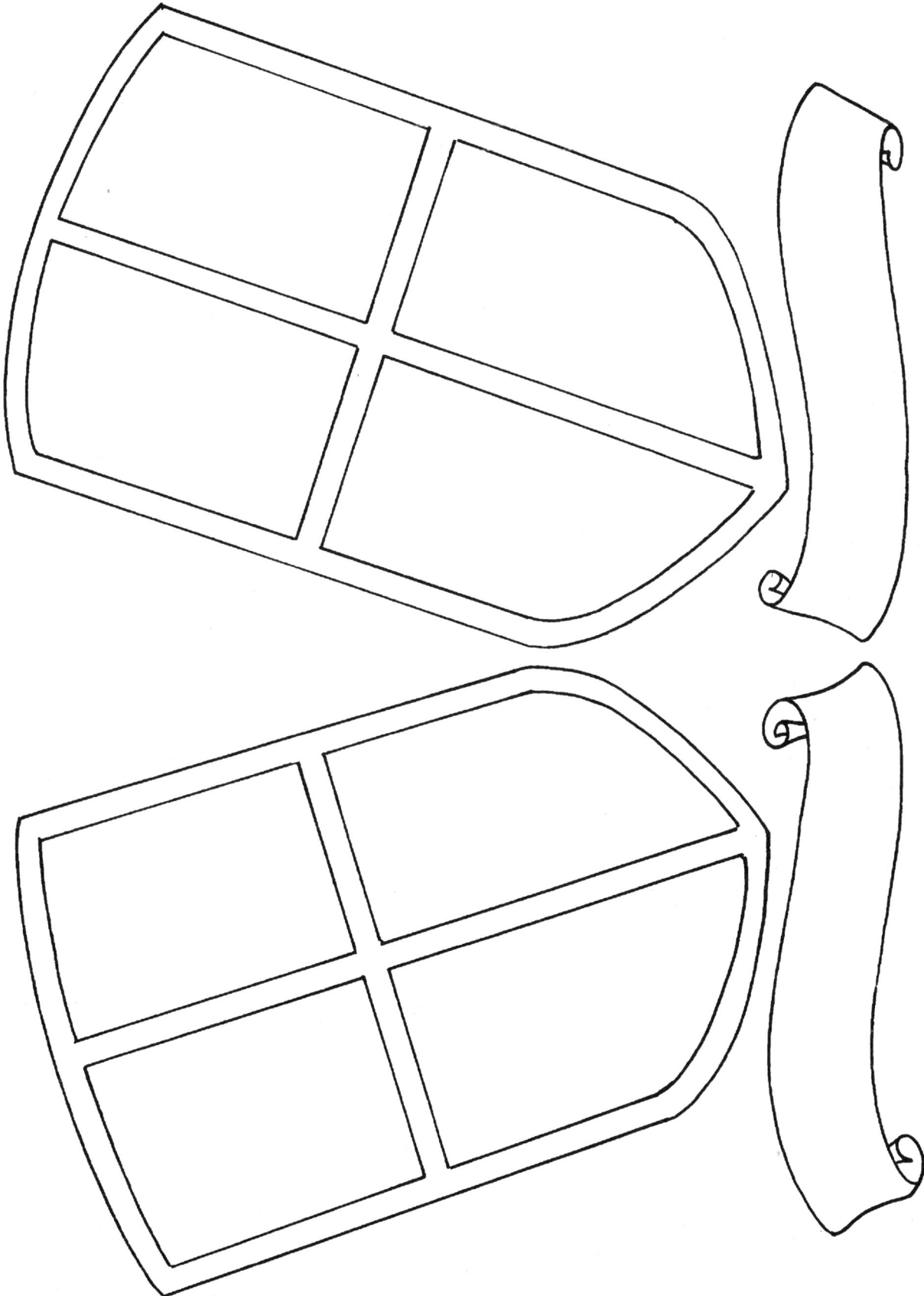

▲ Design a joint coat of arms for your two localities. Write their names in the spaces at the bottom.

Geographical vocabulary (see page 94)

Welcome to earth

Name _____   Date _____

You have come from the planet Mars which is our nearest _____ . At first you landed in the countryside. This _____ area has _____ which are very small and are called_____ . Most people here earn a living through _____ . Larger built up areas are called _____ and very large ones are called _____ . Some of these are now joined together to make very large _____ areas.

The capital city of this _____ is London which is one of the largest in the _____ of Europe. The whole of this area is north of the _____ but the _____ _____ runs through London.

To help you get around you will find it useful to use a _____ . The scale on this will help you work out the _____ between places. If you need to know what _____ you are going in you could use a compass.

Our atmosphere has lots of different kinds of _____. You might get wet if there is heavy _____ and it might be too cold for you to measure the _____ with a _____ .

While you are in the city travel round using our _____ system. You can buy food in a _____ area and enjoy yourself at a park, theatre or other _____ place. As you travel round you may see factories and other types of _____ . You may come across churches, mosques and other places of _____ . If you wish to make friends with any Earth people and find out about our homes, look for a _____ area.

Put these words in the correct gaps to help welcome the Martian to Earth.

leisure	continent	distance	cities	industry
settlements	worship	retail	rural	weather
country	thermometer	map	temperature	urban
agriculture	neighbour	direction	rainfall	equator
villages	prime meridian	transport	towns	residential

**GEOGRAPHY
KS2: PLACES**

Symbols and keys 1 (see page 94)

All the fun of the fair

Name _____   Date _____

This is a plan of a fairground. The entrance, paths and activity areas are shown.

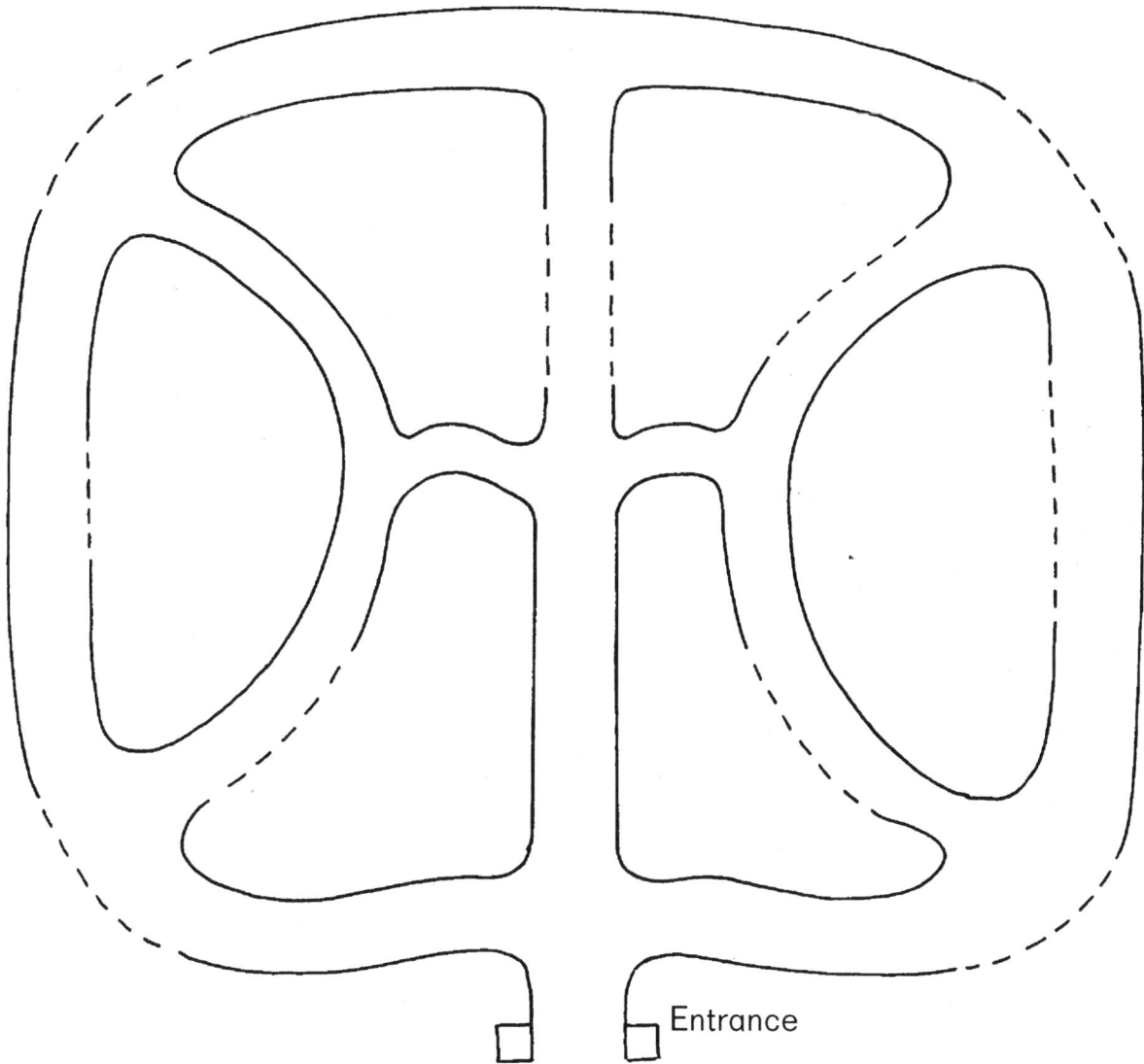

Entrance

▲ Design a key and use symbols on the map for these activities:

My fairground key	Helter skelter	Dodgems
	Coconut shy	Roundabout
	Win a teddy	Ghost train
	Ice cream seller	Fortune teller
	Big wheel	Candyfloss stall

**GEOGRAPHY
KS2: PLACES**

hotocopiables

ymbols and keys 2 (see page 94)

Suburban planner

Name _____   Date _____

▲ You have to plan a new area of suburb.
The motorway and an 'A' road are already shown.

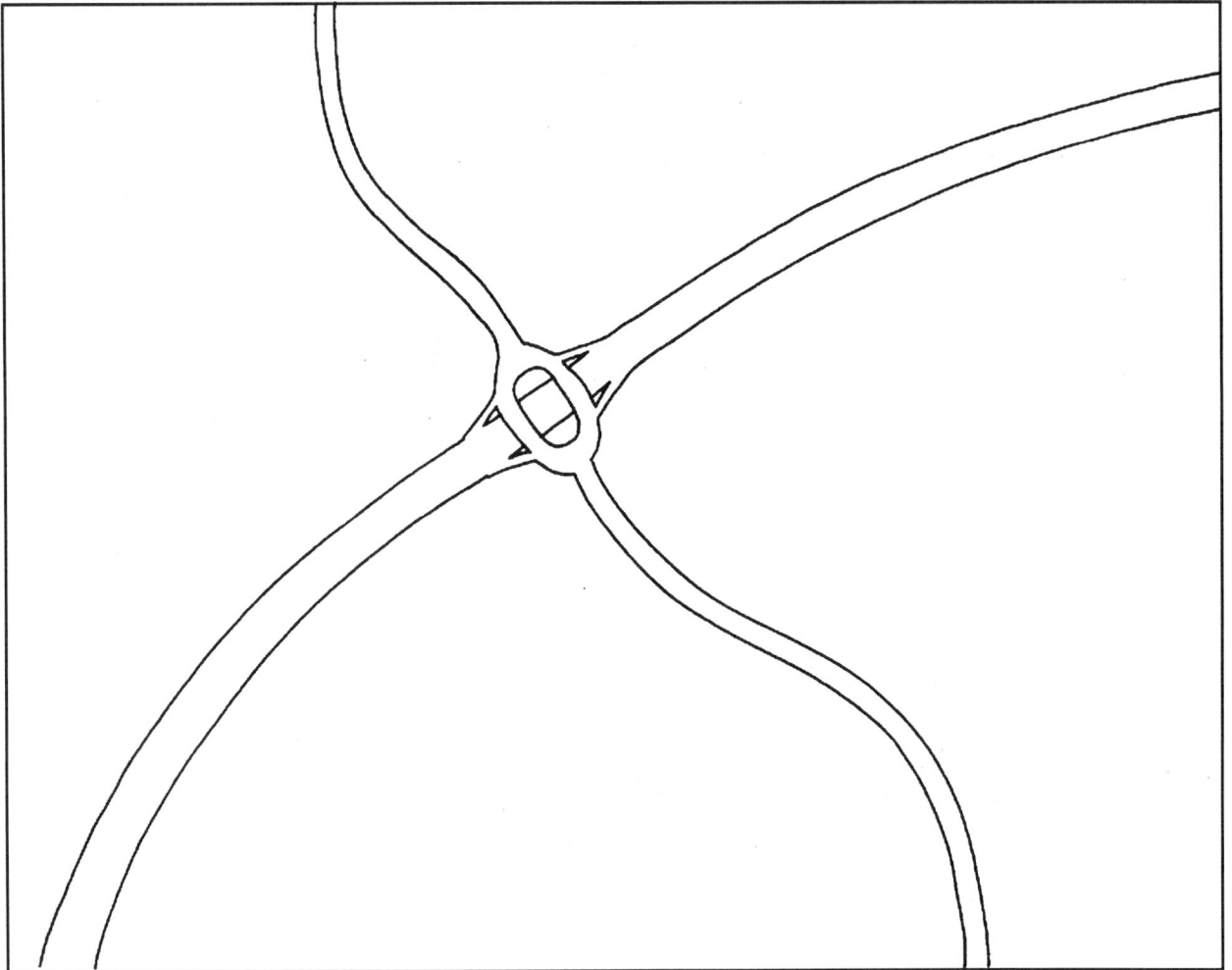

▲ Design your key using Ordnance Survey symbols and put one of each of these features on your map.

My Ordnance Survey key		
	Minor roads	Bridge
	'B' roads	Church with a spire
	'A' roads	Post office
	Motorway	Heliport
	Railway line	Radio mast
	Station	Wind generator

CurriculumBank*
154

EOGRAPHY
KS2: PLACES

Island castle (see page 95)

My Island castle

Name _____   Date _____

You are the owner of a small island off the Scottish coast.
You live in the island's only building, an ancient stone castle.

▲ Draw a map of your island.

▲ Complete the information on scale for each of your maps.

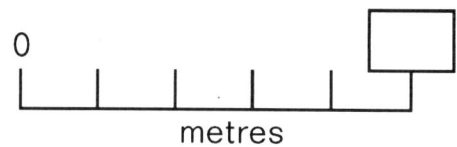

0 [scale bar] metres

One centimetre on the map is .... centimetres on the ground.

1: ....

▲ Draw a map of your castle.

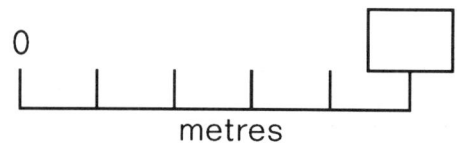

0 [scale bar] metres

One centimetre on the map is .... centimetres on the ground.

1: ....

Which is the larger scale map?

....

**GEOGRAPHY
KS2: PLACES**

Supermarket plan (see page 95)

The plan

Name _____   Date _____

▲ Write the four-figure grid references of the products sold in the old part of the store in the table.

▲ Write the letters for products sold in the new part of the store on the map using the information from the table.

Old part			New part		
v	vegetables		d	drinks	1106
f	fruit		sw	sweets	1306
c	canned food		fr	frozen food	0907
b	biscuits		m	meat	0911
cl	cereals		ch	cheese	0914
fl	flowers		br	bread	1110
s	soups		ck	cake	1112
p	packets		n	newspapers	1315

GEOGRAPHY
KS2: PLACES

Busy ships (see page 96)

Ships ahoy!

Name _____ Date _____

▲ Use the scale and compass direction rose to help you fill in the table.

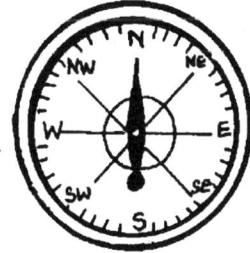

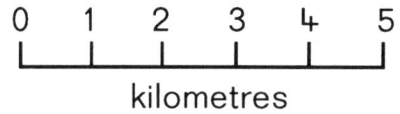

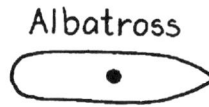

Sea Horse

Guppy

0 1 2 3 4 5
kilometres

Albatross

Kittiwake   Sea Lion   Starfish   Walrus

Porpoise

Dolphin

Sea Horse is ___km___ of Sea Lion	Sea Horse is ___km___ of Sea Lion
Walrus is ___km___ of Sea Lion	Walrus is ___km___ of Sea Lion
Porpoise is ___km___ of Sea Lion	Porpoise is ___km___ of Sea Lion
Albatross is ___km___ of Sea Lion	Albatross is ___km___ of Sea Lion

INFORMATION TECHNOLOGY WITHIN GEOGRAPHY AT KEY STAGE 2

New software related to the National Curriculum – Geography – Places and Themes – appears regularly, particularly in the area of CD-ROMs and teachers may want to supplement the activities with these or other specific software as they become available. The Internet also provides a rich resource base for information and pictures about localities in the UK and further afield.

Main IT focus

The main emphasis for the development of IT capability within these activities is on communicating and handling information.

CD-ROMs

There are an ever growing number of CD-ROMs available for schools which can be used to support work in Geography at Key Stage 2. Two kinds of CD-ROM are likely to be the most useful.

The first are those which provide an encyclopaedic environment. The CD-ROM will contain text, pictures – sometimes in the form of brief movie clips – and sounds such as music, sound effects and speech. Some of these CD-ROMs support work in commercially produced contrasting locality packs.

Children may access information through an index leading to different sections, such as weather or rivers. Others have a simple search for the topic they are interested in; for example, typing the words *rain forest*, will take them to the relevant part of the CD-ROM. When they read the page they may find some of the words highlighted in a different colour. By clicking on these words they will be taken to another section which has more, or linked, information. Moving from one part to another via these 'hot links' is called browsing.

CD-ROM encyclopaedias and atlases provide varying levels of detailed information. There is usually such a vast quantity of information that it is important to try any new CD-ROM in advance of the children using it. Check the quality and relevance of the information, the readability of text, where and how the information can be found and whether it is possible to extract pictures or text for use in other work.

The other type of CD-ROM available is in the form of a collection of pictures which can be used within the children's own work. The *Landscapes* series by Longman Logotron is a good example.

Schools can make their own CD-ROM picture collections to support locality studies. Photographs taken by the school can be put on to a KODAK CD-ROM by taking them to a

chemist. A set of 36 pictures can be transferred on to the CD-ROM at a reasonable cost, with a maximum capacity of 100 pictures.

Ordnance Survey maps

Most Local Education Authorities hold a licence for Ordnance Survey (OS) maps which extends to school use. There are several different formats of maps, but the most useful are the 'Land Line' series which gives a map which can be scaled up and down using appropriate software. The map is ideal for local study work as it shows the position of each house, field and piece of street furniture. Many LEA advisory services have arrangements for getting access to these maps for a minimal handling charge. As the maps can be purchased from the Ordnance Survey, schools can get access to contrasting UK locality maps which lie outside their LEA.

Once you have the maps you will need suitable software for printing and manipulating them on your computer. The available software ranges from a simple map importer which allows you to import the maps into a drawing package, such as *Draw* for RISCOS computers, to a fully working mapping package such as *Aegis 2* from the Advisory Unit for Computers in Education. An important use for such software is the ability to print out sections of the map, appropriate for classroom use, at suitable scales for the age of the children and the task to be undertaken.

Multi-media authoring software

This software is a recent addition for most schools but is proving to be a very versatile and powerful medium. It combines many of the features of a word processor or desktop publishing package, however, it can also link together the different pages of a child's work. Depending on the way that the links are created children can move to different parts of the presentation by simply clicking with a mouse on a symbol, word or picture. Such presentations usually begin with a title page which allow the user to move to different sections of a presentation.

Another important feature is the software's ability to handle a range of different information including text, pictures from art and drawing packages, digitised pictures from scanned images, ion cameras and video cameras, sounds from audio CDs or sound samples and even moving pictures taken from a CD-ROM or captured using a video camera. Some of these latter areas require specialised equipment but the mixing of text, pictures and simple recorded sounds can be undertaken with the minimal amount of equipment. The data files created by such work can be very large and a computer with a hard disk and large memory is needed. Children will need support when they first start to put their ideas into the computer. They will need to know how to create frames, alter text styles, add colours, import graphics and sound files from other disks, and make the links between different pages.

IT links

The grids below relate to the activities in this book to specific areas of IT and to relevant software resources. Activities are referenced by page number. (Bold page numbers indicate activities which have expanded IT content.) The software listed in the second grid is a selection of programs generally available to primary schools, and is not intended as a recommended list. The software featured should be available from most good educational software retailers.

AREA OF IT	SOFTWARE	ACTIVITIES (PAGE NOS.)				
		CHAPTER 1	CHAPTER 2	CHAPTER 3	CHAPTER 4	CHAPTER 5
Communicating Information	Word Processor	14, 15	33, 42	53	69	87, 89, 90
Communicating Information	DTP	14	39, 44	53, **58**, 62		90
Communicating Information	Art software		25	63	74	91
Communicating Information	Drawing software		24, 25, **42**, 44	50, 62	73, 76	85, 90, 91
Communicating Information	Authoring software		39, 42, 44	50, 52	71	
Communicating/ Handling Information	KODAK CD-ROM			50, 52, **58**, 62	67	
Information Handling	Database			55, 57		
Information Handling	CD-ROM		33, 44	62	66, 79	82, 83
Information Handling	Spreadsheet	14, 17, **20**			77, 79	
Information Handling	Graphing software	20		55, 57	77	
Information Handling	OS Map software		27, 37			
Information Handling	Internet		**44**		67	82, 87
Control	ROAMER/PIPP		35			
Control	Tape Recorder	14, 15			71	
Monitoring	Data-logging	17				

SOFTWARE TYPE	BBC/MASTER	RISCOS	NIMBUS/186	WINDOWS	MACINTOSH
Word Processor	Pendown Folio	Pendown Desk Top Folio	All Write Write On	Word for Windows Kid Works 2 Creative Writer	Kid Works 2 Easy Works Creative Writer
DTP	Front Page Extra	Desk Top Folio Pendown DTP Impression Style	Front Page Extra NewSPAper	Creative Writer NewSPAper	Creative Writer
Art Package	Image	Ist Paint Kid Pix Splash	PaintSpa	Colour Magic Kid Pix 2 Fine Artist	Kid Pix 2 Flying Colours Fine Artist
Drawing Software		Draw Vector Art Works		Claris Works Oak Draw	Claris Works
Multi-media Authoring		Magpie Hyperstudio Genesis		Genesis Hyperstudio Illuminus	Hyperstudio
Spreadsheet	Grasshopper Pigeonhole	Grasshopper Advantage Key Count	Grasshopper	Excel starting Grid Claris Works Sparks	Claris Works
Database	Grass	Junior Pinpoint Find IT KeyNote	Grass	Sparks Claris Works Information Workshop	Claris Works Easy Work

GEOGRAPHY
KS2: PLACES

Cross-curricular links

	ENGLISH	MATHEMATICS	SCIENCE	HISTORY	D & T	IT	ART	MUSIC	PE	RE
GEOGRAPHICAL SKILLS IN THE STUDY OF PLACES	Use of appropriate geographical vocabulary. Locational, directional and descriptive words and nouns. Place names as nouns. Reading skills when using secondary sources. Writing directions.	Measuring time and distance, counting and graphicacy skills in fieldwork. Shape and space work in the environment. Data collection, handling and presentation skills during and following field activity.	Fieldwork activity involving scientific processes. Observation, analysis and recording in the field. Geographical data from scientific secondary sources.	Geographical vocabulary and its relevance to historical description. Historical sources to explain features in fieldwork. Using the past to explain the present. Joint historical and geographical enquiry in field.	Identifying design opportunities in the community and the wider human environment as an issues-based field activity. Design issues in the classroom and the school. Presenting proposals.	Laptop computers and data logging equipment used in the field. Computers used to handle, analyse and present data. Communications and media technologies and their role as a secondary source.	Use visual appreciation in learning about physical/human features in the field or through secondary sources. Understand the aesthetic qualities of the environment. Recognise art from the locality/ other cultures.	Listening for sounds in fieldwork environments. Listening to how music represents places and activities in the world.	Vocabulary of movement. Improvement of spatial ability.	Geographical vocabulary and religious stories. Fieldwork which may include visits to religious sites. Records kept by religious organisations (eg. parish records) as a data source.
MAPPING PLACES	Reading maps and keys. Reading directions as a part of following a route. Writing as a part of map making. Labelling keys. Handwriting as important in cartographic precision.	Shape and plan view. Measuring and scaling down. Grids and co-ordinates. Representing 3D shapes as 2D shapes. Area as a part of mapping work. Use of angles in mapping and showing direction on a map.	Mapping the Earth and the place of the Earth as a planet in the solar system. Rotation of the Earth and the poles, equator, prime meridian.	Using old maps to gather information on places. Using maps to illustrate change through time. Using map-making skills to depict places in the past.	The making and using of maps, including thematic maps as a part of producing design proposals for community and environmental projects. Designing 3D maps.	Using graphics and design programs to make maps. Using CD-ROM and other computer atlases and mapping programs. Accessing mapped information from the Internet. On-line commercial map services.	Use control of tools and techniques when drawing maps. Appreciate the aesthetic qualities of mapped images. The plan view as one perspective for the artist. Scaling up/down as a geographical and artistic skill.	Mapping sounds in the environment. Orchestra plans and mapping the performance of music.	Representation of position and movement in physical space. Use of apparatus plans in gymnastics, and pitch and court plans in games. Use of maps in adventurous activities in the outdoor environment.	Mapping world religions. Maps in the study of religious stories.
STUDYING YOUR OWN LOCALITY / CONTRASTING LOCALITIES IN THE UK AND OVERSEAS	Describing localities and listening to descriptions. Adjectives to describe the environment. Reading resource materials and reading in the environment. Making/listening to weather broadcasts.	Estimating size when describing physical/human features. Area and scale work in land/building use mapping. Time in weather work on the seasons.	Physical features and the processes acting on them. Classifying features. Scientific measurement of the weather. Building materials and their qualities.	How the character of localities has changed through time. Establishing the chronology of local places studied. Study units on local history linked with local area study. Past uses of land and buildings.	The aesthetics of a locality and designing the human environment. Design as an issue in localities being studied. Model-making as a way of designing environments. Designing and making models of localities.	Using graphics, word processing and desktop publishing (DTP) applications to present work on physical, human/ environmental issues. Presenting views through use of video and DTP newspapers. TV/ video/radio/ Internet sources.	Aesthetic qualities of environments. Understanding what gives 'character' in a place. Recognise visual elements of space, pattern, shape, line and form in different places. Recognise genres/styles of art in places studied.	The musical culture and traditions of different places. Music which creates or recreates the atmosphere of a place.	Leisure, sport and recreation as part of the service sector in the human world. Effect of these facilities on the use of land. Comparisons in health and sports, leisure and recreation between different localities.	Religious land and buildings in the human environment. Land use issues and religious sites. Comparisons in religious tradition and the importance of religion in everyday life in different localities.